Better Homes and Gardens®

embroidery

Favorites from the Editors of
AMERICAN PATCHWORK &
QUILTING®

Better Homes and Gardens® Crafts Group
Des Moines, Iowa

Editorial Content Chief	LINDA AUGSBURG
Group Editorial Leader	DOUG KOUMA
Assistant Managing Editor	JENNIFER SPEER RAMUNDT

Better Homes and Gardens
embroidery

Senior Editor ELIZABETH TISINGER BEESE
Editors JILL ABELOE MEAD AND JODY SANDERS
Assistant Editor LISA SCHUMACHER
Assistant Multimedia Editor LINDSAY FULLINGTON
Contributing Technical Editor LISA FLYR
Contributing Copy Editors ANGELA INGLE AND MARY HELEN SCHILTZ

Design Director NANCY WILES
Assistant Art Director ELIZABETH STUMBO
Contributing Graphic Designer CAN WICASTA CREATIVE
Contributing Illustrators GLENDA ALDRICH, SHAWN DRAFAHL, ALISON GAMM, BARB GORDON, LIZ GORDON, CHRIS NEUBAUER, AND ANN WEISS
Contributing Project Designer HEIDI PALKOVIC
Administrative Assistant LORI EGGERS
Vice President/Group Publisher SCOTT MORTIMER

Prepress Desktop Specialist	TONY JUNGWEBER
Color Quality Analyst	TONY HUNT
Director, Meredith Photo Studios	BOB FURSTENAU
Consumer Marketing Director	LIZ BREDESON
Business Director	JANICE CROAT

Meredith National Media Group
President TOM HARTY

EXECUTIVE VICE PRESIDENTS
President, Media Sales	RICHARD PORTER
President, Parents Network	CAREY WITMER
President, Women's Lifestyle	THOMAS WITSCHI
President, Meredith Digital	JON WERTHER
Meredith Home Group	JAMES CARR
Creative Content Leader	GAYLE GOODSON BUTLER
Chief Marketing Officer	NANCY WEBER
Chief Revenue Officer	MICHAEL BROWNSTEIN
General Manager	DOUG OLSON

SENIOR VICE PRESIDENTS
Chief Digital Officer	ANDY WILSON
Digital Sales	CAROLYN BEKKEDAHL
Research Solutions	BRITTA CLEVELAND

VICE PRESIDENTS
Business Planning and Analysis	ROB SILVERSTONE
Consumer Marketing	JANET DONNELLY
Corporate Marketing	STEPHANIE CONNOLLY
Corporate Sales	BRIAN KIGHTLINGER
Digital Video	LAURA ROWLEY
Direct Media	PATTI FOLLO
Brand Licensing	ELISE CONTARSY
Communications	PATRICK TAYLOR
Human Resources	DINA NATHANSON
Strategic Sourcing, Newsstand, Production	CHUCK HOWELL

meredith

Chairman and Chief Executive Officer STEPHEN M. LACY
President, Meredith Local Media Group PAUL KARPOWICZ

Vice Chairman MELL MEREDITH FRAZIER
In Memoriam — E. T. MEREDITH III (1933-2003)

For editorial questions: *American Patchwork & Quilting,* 1716 Locust St., LN-204, Des Moines, IA 50309-3023; apq@meredith.com

from the EDITOR

Embroidery. It's everywhere. Whether adorning home decor, holiday projects, or fashion accessories, colorful stitches can transform myriad everyday items. For many creative spirits, hand embroidery is also a relaxing escape from day-to-day stressors, allowing them to change something ordinary into something exquisite, funky, or whimsical—it all depends on the design and colors chosen.

Historically, part of what makes embroidery so appealing is the ability to personalize the design. You can change colors, use a different stitch, or modify the pattern to create something entirely new and entirely you. Embroidery allows you to express your vision, stitch by stitch. Are you the type that is driven by the process and joy of stitching? In these pages you'll find projects to keep you busy in the hours set aside for "you" time. Or maybe you're the stitcher who wants to conquer and perfect every type of embroidery. There's certainly much to learn, including ribbon embroidery, needlepunch, cross-stitch, embroidered appliqué, and many traditional stitches. Still, some embroiderers feel bliss only when they hear the "oohs" and "aahs" from friends and family over their finished creations.

Whether your first embroidery project was completed during your childhood, or whether a project chosen from this book will be your first attempt, it's okay if you don't know a stem stitch from a backstitch. Every stitch you need to create the projects in this book is included in its pages. For a refresher, start at the back. The Basics section (beginning on *page 148*) includes 13 stitches, illustrated and photographed, along with step-by-step instructions to help you learn or review each stitch. In addition, there's information on transferring patterns, beginning and ending a stitch, and much more, so you can create any project with confidence.

The three chapters in this book provide an exciting variety of projects to inspire you. There are classically elegant items and whimsical embroidered wood pieces that you'll be proud to showcase in every room of the house. For the holidays, we've included delightful Christmas ornaments and decorations, a spring penny rug, and Halloween and fall projects. In our Gifts chapter, you'll find accessories—a simple scarf, a charming necklace, a kitschy brooch, and a vintage-look headband— plus spa-inspired accents and gifts for family, friends, and fellow stitchers.

So slow down, explore your creative side, and get started on your next embroidery project!

Linda

Linda Augsburg
Editorial Content Chief

contents

home

holiday

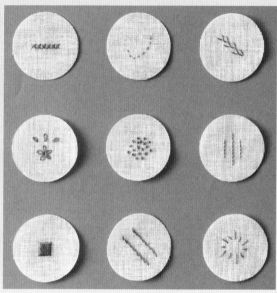

gifts

basics

bonus!

We've provided
full-size embroidery patterns
for several designs from our chapter
dividers; see *Pattern Sheet 2.*

HOME

Embroidery is everywhere in home decorating. But rather than purchase mass-produced accessories, stitch your own custom projects with these ideas for nearly every room.

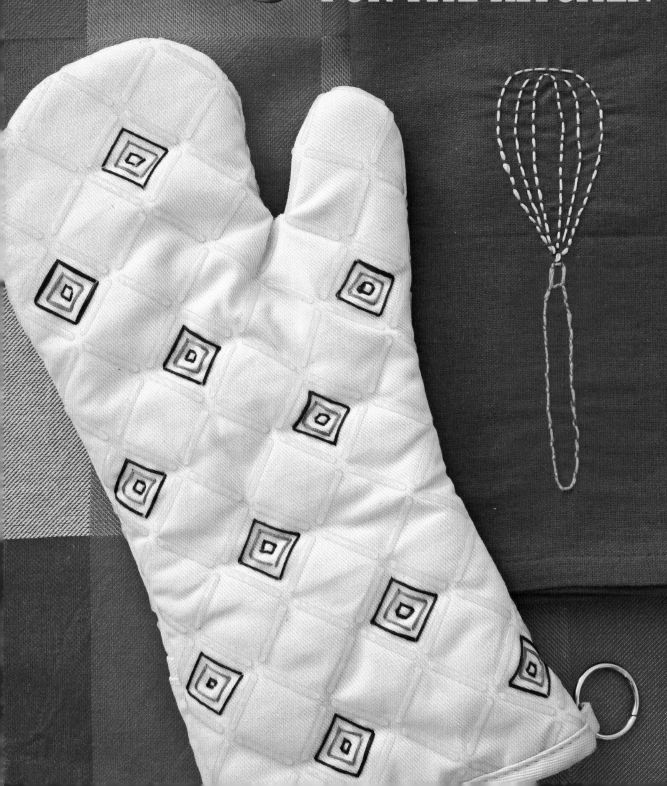

stitches
FOR THE KITCHEN

Start with solid-color kitchen linens, then add fun patterns using just three beginner embroidery stitches.

DESIGNER **SÄRAH GOLDSCHADT**

materials

- Kitchen linens: tea towel, oven mitt, apron, and napkin
- Tracing paper
- Transfer paper
- Embroidery floss: light blue, pink, dark red, yellow, white, light green
- Embroidery needle

embroider linens

Refer to Basic Stitches, beginning on *page 154*, for running stitch, stem stitch, and backstitch instructions. Use four strands of embroidery floss for all stitches.

1 Transfer the desired Full-Size Embroidery Pattern from *Pattern Sheet 1* to a pressed linen of your choice using tracing and transfer paper, positioning the designs on the fabric as desired.

2 For the tea towel, *opposite,* use light blue floss and running stitches for the whisk beater. Use pink floss to stem-stitch the handle.

3 For the oven mitt, *opposite,* use the silicone grip motif printed on the fabric as a guide for your stitching (this will vary based on your own oven mitt). Use dark red floss to backstitch the outer and inner squares, and use pink floss to backstitch the center square.

4 For the apron, *above right,* stitch all the motifs with running stitches. Use yellow floss for the mixer and the spatula, and use white floss for the beaters. Use light green floss for the bowl.

5 For the napkin, *right,* use white floss and running stitches for the spoon, knife, and fork.

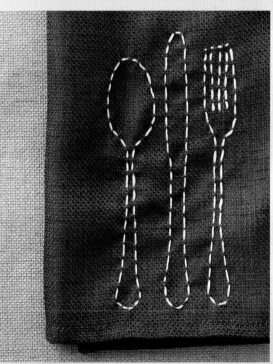

sweet **botanical**

With its spindly form and distinctive round blooms,
the sarsaparilla plant comes to life with textural crewel stitches.

DESIGNER **KATHERINE SHAUGHNESSEY**

materials

- 1½ yards natural linen (pillow top, pillow back)
- ⅝ yard muslin (lining)
- Air- or water-soluble fabric pen
- Crewel wool thread: red-orange, three shades of orange, cream, aqua
- Chenille needle, size 24 (or comparable crewel needle)
- 18"-square pillow form

Finished pillow: 18" square

Yardages and cutting instructions are based on 42" of usable fabric width. **Measurements** include ½" seam allowances. Sew with right sides together unless otherwise stated.

cut fabrics

Cut pieces in the following order.

From natural linen, cut:
- 1—24" square
- 2—23×19" rectangles

From muslin, cut:
- 1—19" square

embroider pillow top

Refer to Basic Stitches, beginning on *page 154*, for chain stitch, split stitch, and French knot instructions. Wrap floss around needle two times for a double-wrapped French knot and four times for a quadruple-wrapped French knot.

1   Using a light box or bright window, center and trace the Full-Size Embroidery Pattern on *Pattern Sheet 3* onto the natural linen 24" square with the fabric pen to make embroidery foundation.

2   Use red-orange thread to chain-stitch the stem and branches. Split-stitch the leaves, choosing one shade of orange thread for each leaf. Use cream thread to stitch each flower with a circular couching stitch (see instructions on *page 13*) and double-wrapped French knots on the ends. Use aqua thread to make a quadruple-wrapped French knot in each flower center.

3   Block the embroidered foundation. (For details, see *page 159*.) Trim to 19" square including seam allowances to make the pillow top.

finish pillow

1. Place the muslin 19" square on wrong side of pillow top. Baste pieces together ¼" from all edges to line the pillow top.

2. With wrong sides inside, fold each natural linen 23×19" rectangle in half to form two double-thick 11½×19" rectangles. (The double thickness makes the pillow back more stable.) Overlap folded edges by about 4" to make a 19" square (**Pillow Back Assembly Diagram**). Baste around entire square to make pillow back.

3. Layer pillow back and lined pillow top with right sides together. Sew together around all edges. Clip corners and turn

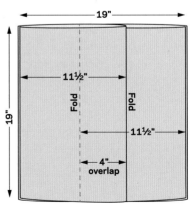

PILLOW BACK ASSEMBLY DIAGRAM

right side out to make pillow cover. Insert pillow form to complete the pillow.

Circular Couching Stitch

1 To make a circular couching stitch, sew a series of straight stitches so that one end of each stitch touches the edge of a marked arch or circle.

2 Lace the thread underneath the straight stitches and pull it through to form a circle.

3 Bring your needle up next to the center of one of the straight stitches (A), bring the thread over the straight stitch, then go back down on the other side of the stitch (B) to tack down the straight stitch. Repeat on each straight stitch.

4 Lace the thread underneath each straight stitch, on the outside of each Step 3 stitch. Pull the thread through to form an outer circle.

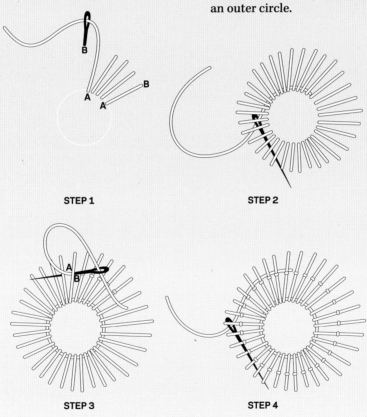

STEP 1

STEP 2

STEP 3

STEP 4

CIRCULAR COUCHING STITCH

let there be *light*

Chain-stitched swirls in orange, blue, and lavender add a punch of color to a plain white lampshade.

DESIGNER **BRENDA DRAKE LESCH**

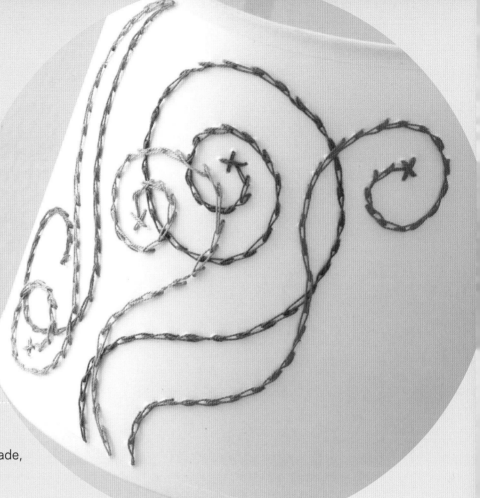

materials

- Smooth-sided white lampshade, about 4" tall
- Pencil
- Awl
- Perle cotton No. 8: orange, blue, lavender
- Tapestry needle

embroider lampshade

Refer to Basic Stitches, beginning on *page 154,* for chain stitch and cross-stitch instructions.

1　Place the Full-Size Embroidery Pattern, *right,* inside the lampshade and tape the pattern in place along the top and bottom of shade. Use a pencil to lightly trace the design onto the shade front. Remove the pattern.

2　Use an awl to carefully punch holes approximately ¼" apart along the marked lines.

3　Using a tapestry needle, chain-stitch each swirl using orange, blue, or lavender perle cotton (see photo, *above*). Add a matching cross-stitch at the end of each swirl to complete the lampshade.

Chain stitch

Cross-stitch

Let There Be Light
Full-Size Embroidery Pattern

love note

A wreath of cherries and a subtle "I Love You" combine to form this lovely redwork pillow. DESIGNER **ALEX ANDERSON**

materials

- 2⅛ yards muslin (embroidery foundation, pillow cover)
- ⅛ yard red print (piping)
- Air- or water-soluble fabric pen
- 23" square tracing paper
- Embroidery floss: red and ecru
- Embroidery needle
- 18"-square pillow form

Finished pillow: 23" square

Yardages and cutting instructions are based on 42" of usable fabric width. **Measurements** include ¼" seam allowances. Sew with right sides together unless otherwise stated.

cut fabrics

Cut pieces in the following order.

From muslin, cut:
- 1—23½×52" rectangle
- 1—19½" square

From red print, cut:
- 2—1×42" strips

prepare embroidery foundation

1 The Full-Size Embroidery Pattern is on *Pattern Sheet 1*. Lay tracing paper over the pattern and trace all lines, including the placement guides. Referring to **Embroidery Placement Diagram**, rotate tracing paper over the cherry wreath portion of the design to make the wreath tracing guide.

EMBROIDERY PLACEMENT DIAGRAM

2 Fold muslin 19½" square in half vertically and horizontally. Lightly finger-press each fold to create an embroidery foundation with placement guides; unfold.

3 Place the wreath tracing guide on a light box or bright window. Lay the embroidery foundation atop wreath tracing guide, aligning creases on the foundation with placement guides on the tracing paper. Using an air- or water-soluble fabric pen, trace the design onto the embroidery foundation.

embroider pillow top

Refer to Basic Stitches, beginning on *page 154*, for stem stitch and French knot instructions. Use two strands of embroidery floss for all stitches.

1 Using red floss, stem-stitch the wreath.

2 With ecru floss, stem-stitch the lettering *I Love You.*

3 Using ecru floss, add French knots to the lettering as shown on the pattern.

4 Lay embroidered foundation facedown on a terry cloth towel and press. (The towel prevents the stitches from getting flattened during pressing.) Trim embroidered foundation to 18½" square to make the pillow top.

finish pillow

1 Cut and piece red print 1×42" strips to make an 83"-long strip.

2 With wrong side inside, fold and press the red print strip in half lengthwise to make a ½"-wide piping strip. Aligning raw edges, sew the piping strip to the pillow top, mitering corners. Turn under and press the seam allowances toward wrong side of the pillow top.

3 Fold short edges of muslin 23½×52" rectangle under ½". Turn same edges under ½" again; press. Using a ⅜" seam allowance, stitch along the short edges to hem.

4 With right side inside, fold hemmed edges to center, overlapping them by 4", to make a 23×23½" rectangle (**Pillow Cover Diagram**).

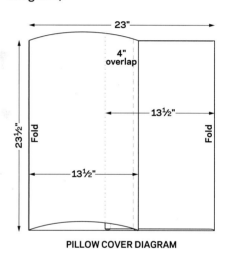

PILLOW COVER DIAGRAM

5 Sew together raw edges to make the pillow cover; turn right side out.

6 Place the pillow cover with opening side down. Center the piped pillow top on pillow cover. Pin in place.

7 Topstitch in the ditch through all layers between the pillow top and piping to create a flange edge. Insert the pillow form through the back opening to complete the pillow.

tip >
When stitching with red embroidery floss on light-color fabric, be mindful of the back of your work. To prevent show-through, try to work neatly by running your stitches through the backs of previous stitches or switching to a freshly threaded needle when stitching a new area.

ribbon *beauty*

Turn ready-made basics into pretty floral heirlooms with vibrant silk ribbon.

DESIGNER **VICTORIA BROWN**

THIS PAGE: Embellish a damask runner with ribbon hearts and flowers to enhance your home decor.
OPPOSITE, TOP: Use a Victorian-style initial rubber stamp to create a pillow-top template for embroidered ribbon roses, buds, and leaves.
OPPOSITE, BOTTOM LEFT: Stitch fresh-faced pansies to adorn a set of special-occasion napkins.
OPPOSITE, BOTTOM RIGHT: Gussy up linen cocktail napkins with rings of posies stitched along the edges.

for all projects

Before you begin, see "Silk Ribbon Embroidery Tips" on *page 25*.

Thread the chenille needle with a 20" length of 4-millimeter ribbon in the color indicated; needle-lock the ribbon. To lock the ribbon, thread the needle, pulling about 3" of ribbon through the eye. Pierce the 3" piece ½" from the end. Pull the long piece of ribbon, taking up the slack, until the knot slides to the end of the needle eye. To end the ribbon, knot on the back side and cut beyond the knot.

For 7-millimeter ribbon, thread the chenille needle with a 16" length of the indicated color. Do not needle-lock or knot this wide ribbon;

leave a ½"–1" tail on the back side to start and end the ribbon. When the embroidery is complete, secure the ribbon ends on back side by tacking them in place with sewing thread.

Refer to "Ribbon Embroidery 101" on *page 26* for a basic primer on making the ribbon embroidery stitches used in these projects.

To press the completed embroidery, place the design facedown on a terry cloth towel. Hover a steam iron over the back of the embroidery and press very lightly. If any stitches are crushed when pressing, touch the ribbon with a wet cotton swab to rejuvenate.

Table Runner

(shown *above* and on *page 20*)

materials

- White damask table runner
- Water-soluble fabric pen
- Water-soluble stabilizer
- Extra-fine-point permanent marker: black
- 4-millimeter silk ribbon: light pink, dark pink, yellow, green
- Buttonhole silk-twist thread: green
- Needles: embroidery and chenille, size 20

embroider table runner

1. Fold one end of the table runner in half lengthwise and place several marks along the fold with a water-soluble fabric pen to indicate the center of the runner.

2. Trace the Table Runner Embroidery Pattern on *page 27* onto water-soluble stabilizer with the permanent marker. Place the stabilizer pattern on the front of the table runner, centering the pattern on the marked end of the runner; pin in place. Baste the pattern to the runner. All embroidery will be through both the stabilizer and the runner. Place the runner in an embroidery hoop if desired, taking care not to tear the stabilizer.

3. Starting at the bottom of the design, use light pink ribbon to make single-wrapped French knots, loosely wrapping the ribbon one time around the needle. Complete all the light pink French knots on the pattern.

4. To create each flower, use dark pink ribbon to make six to 10 lazy daisy stitches, leaving the center open. Knot and cut the ribbon at the end of each flower before continuing on to the next. Add four or five single-wrapped French knots at the center of each flower with yellow ribbon, loosely wrapping the ribbon one time around the needle.

5. Thread the embroidery needle with a 20" length of green silk-twist thread; knot the end. Stem-stitch the leaf stems; knot the thread when stems are complete. For the leaves, make lazy daisy stitches with green ribbon.

6. Remove the basting stitches from the stabilizer and trim away as much stabilizer as possible. Blot the ribbon embroidery with a wet cloth to remove any stabilizer underneath the stitches. Allow the runner to dry.

7. Repeat steps 1–6 on the opposite end to complete the table runner.

Initial Pillow

(shown *above right* and on *page 21*)

materials
- Teal douppioni silk pillow
- Initial rubber stamp
- Water-soluble fabric pen
- Permanent ink pad
- Water-soluble stabilizer
- Buttonhole silk-twist thread: green
- 4-millimeter silk ribbon: pink, light mauve, deep mauve, pale yellow, purple, pale blue, variegated green
- Embroidery floss: pink
- 7-millimeter silk ribbon: gold
- Needles: embroidery; chenille, size 20; beading, size 10
- 2-millimeter white or ivory pearl beads
- Beading thread
- Teal sewing thread

embroider pillow

1. Open the seam at the bottom of the pillow and remove the stuffing. Fold the pillow in half lengthwise and crosswise; place several marks along the folds with a water-soluble fabric pen to indicate the center of the pillow. Press the ink pad onto the rubber stamp. When the stamp is properly coated with ink, stamp the initial on the water-soluble stabilizer. Place the stabilizer pattern on the front of the pillow, centering the stamped initial; pin in place. Baste the pattern to the pillow. All embroidery will be through both the stabilizer and the pillow top. Place the pillow front in an embroidery hoop if desired, taking care not to tear the stabilizer.

2. Thread the embroidery needle with a 20" length of green silk-twist thread; knot one end. Stem-stitch the outline of the initial and the small stems, and make leaves with lazy daisy stitches.

3. Using the Initial Pillow Embroidery Pattern on *page 28* as a guide, make woven roses with pink embroidery floss and one or more of the 4-millimeter ribbons in pink, light mauve, or deep mauve. Make the loop stitches with 7-millimeter gold ribbon. Use assorted ribbons and ribbon stitches to make the remaining flowers and buds.

4. Embroider all leaves throughout the initial with ribbon stitches and 4-millimeter variegated green ribbon.

5. Add single-wrapped French knots using all the colors of 4- and 7-millimeter ribbon, loosely wrapping the ribbon around the needle one time.

6. Use beading thread and the beading needle to attach a pearl bead to each gold loop stitch and woven rose.

7. Remove basting stitches from the stabilizer and trim away as much stabilizer as possible. Blot the ribbon embroidery with a wet cloth to remove any stabilizer underneath the stitches. Allow the pillow top to dry. Insert stuffing back into the pillow. Slip-stitch the opening closed with teal sewing thread to complete the pillow.

Pansy Napkin

(shown *above* and on *page 21*)

materials

- White damask napkin
- Water-soluble stabilizer
- Extra-fine-point permanent marker: black
- 7-millimeter silk ribbon: purple and pink
- 4-millimeter silk ribbon: gold, lime green, green
- Buttonhole silk-twist thread: pink, green, lime green
- Needles: embroidery and chenille, size 20
- Lightweight fusible interfacing

embroider pansy napkin

1. Trace the Pansy Napkin Embroidery Pattern on *page 29* onto water-soluble stabilizer with the permanent marker. Place the stabilizer pattern on the front of the napkin, positioning it in one corner as desired; pin in place. Baste the pattern to the napkin. All stitching will be through both the stabilizer and the napkin. Place the napkin in an embroidery hoop if desired, taking care not to tear the stabilizer.

2. Embroider the large pansies one at a time, beginning at the center of the bouquet and working outward. Use 7-millimeter purple ribbon to make six loose straight stitches at the bottom of the pansy, beginning with the center stitch and adding stitches on each side. Make two loose straight stitches with 7-millimeter pink ribbon above the purple stitches. Add a single-wrapped French knot at the center of the flower with 4-millimeter gold ribbon, loosely wrapping the ribbon around the needle one time. Use the embroidery needle to make small straight stitches with pink silk-twist thread on top of the purple ribbon stitches.

3. For the small pansy buds, make small straight stitches with 7-millimeter purple and pink ribbon. Add two small straight stitches to each bud with 4-millimeter green ribbon.

4. Use ribbon stitches to make the larger leaves within the design using the 4-millimeter lime green ribbon on one side of the leaves and the 4-millimeter green ribbon on the remaining side.

5. Using green and lime green silk-twist thread and the embroidery needle, stem-stitch the stems throughout the design, and add small lazy daisy stitches for the leaves on the stems at the center bottom of the design. Make ribbon stitches for the individual leaves on the stems among the flowers with the 4-millimeter lime green and green ribbon.

6. Remove the basting stitches from the stabilizer and trim away as much stabilizer as possible. Blot the embroidery with a wet cloth or cotton swab to remove any stabilizer underneath the stitches.

7. When the napkin is dry, secure the ribbon ends on the back with tack stitches and trim the tails. Cut a piece of lightweight fusible interfacing and fuse over the back of the embroidery to complete the napkin.

Linen Napkin

(shown *opposite* and on *page 21*)

materials

- 6"-square pink linen napkin
- Water-soluble fabric pen
- Buttonhole silk-twist thread: variegated green
- 4-millimeter silk ribbon: pink, yellow, green
- Needles: embroidery and chenille, size 20

Silk Ribbon Embroidery Tips

1 Select any tight even-weave fabric, including moiré, douppioni silk, linen, cotton brocade, velvet, and denim. When stitching on damask, douppioni silk, or linen, use an embroidery hoop. When stitching is completed, remove the hoop to prevent marks on the fabric. Do not use a hoop when adding ribbon embroidery to velvet (to avoid damaging the nap).

2 Always use a chenille needle for ribbon embroidery. Be sure the 4-millimeter silk ribbon is needle-locked (see instructions on *page 22*) into the eye to prevent it from slipping out of the large eye. Trim the ribbon end at a 45° angle before threading. This will create ease in threading the needle and will also prevent the ribbon from fraying.

3 Stitch with 15"–20" lengths of ribbon. This short length produces less stress on the ribbon, which will go through the fabric many times while creating the flowers.

4 Create ribbon embroidery stitches using loose tension. Ribbon embroidery is a dimensional needle art. These projects require loose tension when creating the flowers within the designs.

5 Protect your embroidered piece by fusing a piece of lightweight fusible interfacing to the back of the finished embroidery. This will keep ribbon tails in place and neaten the back side.

embroider linen napkin

1 Use the water-soluble fabric pen to trace around a dime at each corner of the napkin and at the center of each side.

2 Thread the embroidery needle with a 20" length of variegated green silk-twist

thread; knot one end. Using the Linen Napkin Embroidery Pattern on *page 29* as a guide and beginning at the bottom of one circle, stem-stitch around the circle. When the circle is complete, knot and trim the thread. Repeat for each circle.

3 Use pink ribbon to embroider two flowers at the center bottom of each circle. To create a flower, make four or five small straight stitches, approximately ⅛" long, being careful to keep ribbon from twisting. Knot and cut the ribbon when the two flowers are complete. Add a single-wrapped French knot at the center of each flower with yellow ribbon, loosely wrapping ribbon around needle one time.

4 For the leaves, make tiny straight stitches with green ribbon, placing two among the flowers and four pairs around each circle.

5 When the embroidery is complete, remove any visible water-soluble marks with a dampened cotton swab. Trim any ribbon tails on the back to complete the napkin.

Ribbon Embroidery 101

Here's how to re-create the various stitches used on these projects.

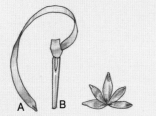

STRAIGHT STITCH

1 Bring up at A; pull through.
2 Insert down at B; pull through.

RIBBON STITCH

1 Bring up at A; pull through.
2 Lay ribbon flat on fabric and insert needle at B, piercing ribbon and pulling through slowly. Ribbon will curl into B, so don't pull tightly or you'll lose the effect. To vary the curl, pierce B to the right or left of center of ribbon width.

STEM STITCH

1 Bring up at A; pull through.
2 Insert needle at B on stem line. Holding ribbon below line, pull out at C directly in line with last stitch (not above or below it) and halfway between A and B; pull through. Continue to end of line, making sure ribbon is always held below the stitching line.

FRENCH KNOT

1 Bring up at A; pull through. Holding ribbon or thread, lay needle on top.
2 Wrap ribbon or thread around needle one to three times. Insert needle at B a thread or two from A. Gently slide wrapped ribbon or thread down the needle to rest against the fabric, and pull through.

WOVEN ROSE

1 Stitch a foundation line of five straight stitches, like the spokes of a wheel, in sewing thread that matches the color of your silk ribbon.
2 Thread the needle with the silk ribbon and, working from the center out, bring the needle up at A and pull through. Weave the ribbon around the spokes by sliding the needle over B and then under C, alternating spokes all around the wheel, without piercing the fabric. Continue weaving until the spokes are full. Pull the ribbon loosely, allowing twists in the ribbon here and there.
3 Bring the needle down at D, pull through, and knot off.

LAZY DAISY

1 Bring up at A; pull through.
2 Make loop in direction of other end of stitch and insert at B a thread or two to side of A. Pull out at C, in direction needle points until loose loop is formed; then stitch back down at D. To prevent ribbon from twisting when it's drawn through fabric after pulling out at C, arrange it around the needle so it's flat. Gently hold in place with your thumb while sliding needle and ribbon through.

LOOP STITCH

1 Bring needle and ribbon up through fabric. Push needle down about ⅛" from entry point. Use your thumb to hold ribbon tight as you pull it through and form a loop.
2 Hold loop in place with your thumb or a blunt needle, and bring the needle back up through the ribbon at the base of the loop.

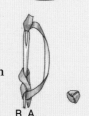

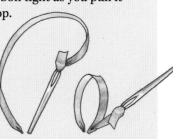

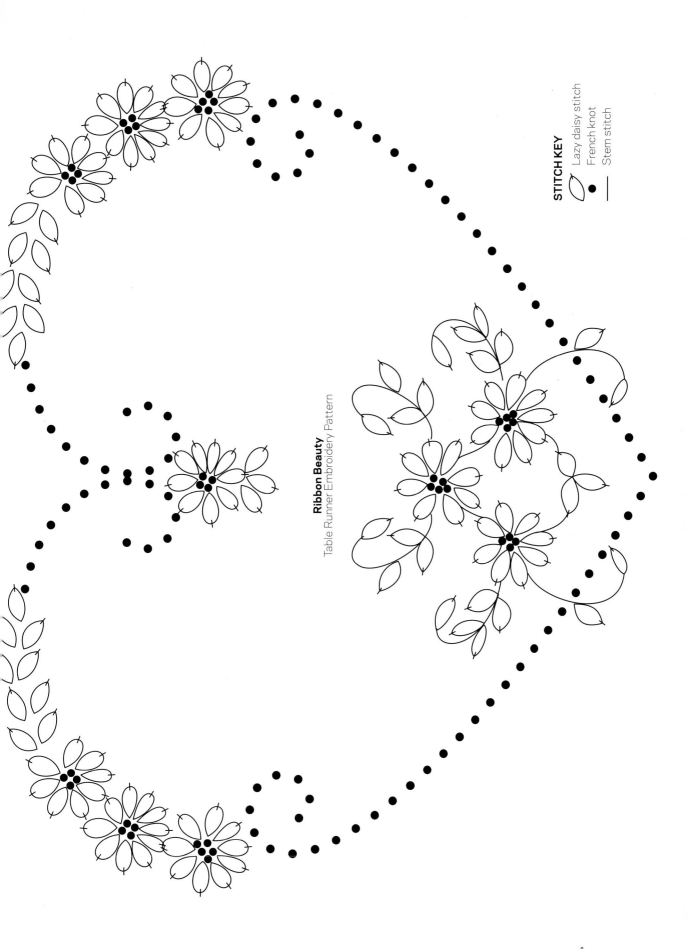

Ribbon Beauty
Table Runner Embroidery Pattern

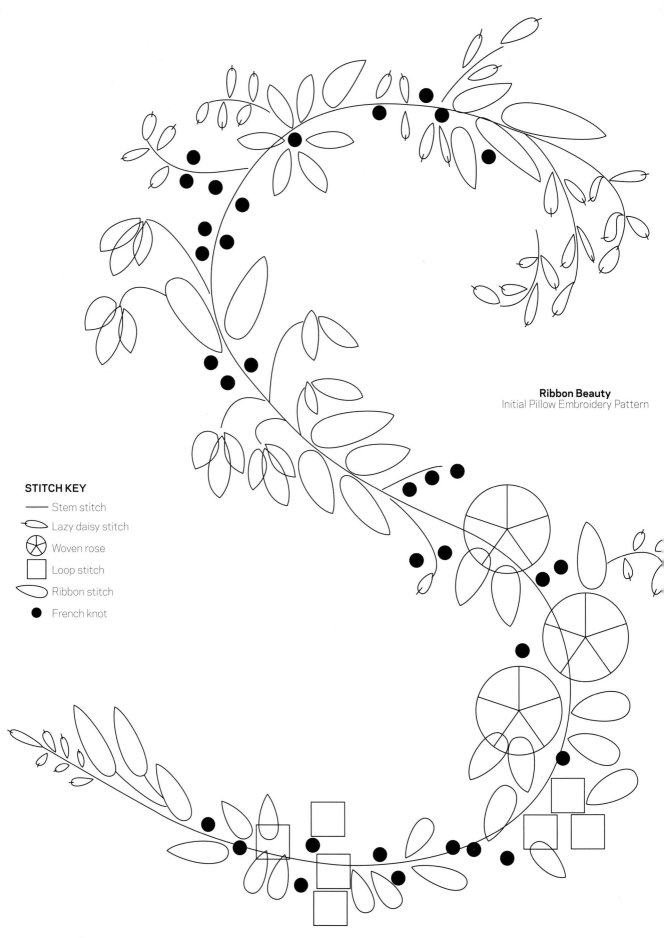

Ribbon Beauty
Initial Pillow Embroidery Pattern

STITCH KEY

— Stem stitch

Lazy daisy stitch

Woven rose

Loop stitch

Ribbon stitch

● French knot

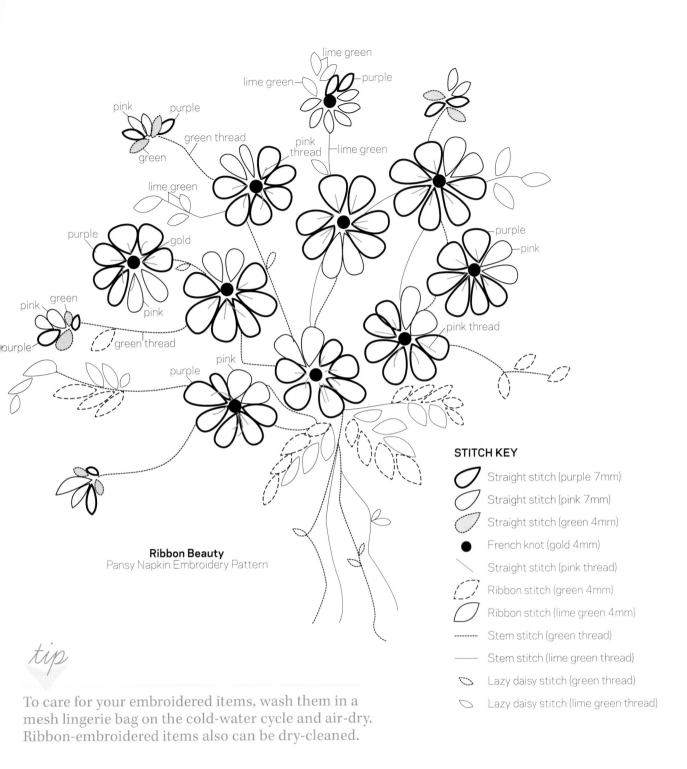

Ribbon Beauty
Pansy Napkin Embroidery Pattern

Labels on pattern: lime green, lime green, purple, lime green, pink, purple, green, green thread, lime green, pink thread, lime green, purple, gold, purple, pink, pink, pink, green, purple, green thread, purple, pink, pink thread, purple

STITCH KEY

Straight stitch (purple 7mm)
Straight stitch (pink 7mm)
Straight stitch (green 4mm)
French knot (gold 4mm)
Straight stitch (pink thread)
Ribbon stitch (green 4mm)
Ribbon stitch (lime green 4mm)
Stem stitch (green thread)
Stem stitch (lime green thread)
Lazy daisy stitch (green thread)
Lazy daisy stitch (lime green thread)

tip

To care for your embroidered items, wash them in a mesh lingerie bag on the cold-water cycle and air-dry. Ribbon-embroidered items also can be dry-cleaned.

Ribbon Beauty
Linen Napkin Embroidery Pattern

STITCH KEY

Stem stitch (variegated green thread)
Straight stitch (pink 4mm)
Straight stitch (green 4mm)
French knot (yellow 4mm)

welcome *cottage*

Bring this fairy tale-inspired scene to life with appliquéd wool and red embroidery stitches. DESIGNER **JANET CARIJA BRANDT**

materials

- ⅜ yard cream felted wool (appliqué foundation, appliqués)
- 9×21" piece (fat eighth) red stripe (binding)
- 18×21" piece (fat quarter) backing fabric
- 12×15" lightweight batting
- Freezer paper
- Embroidery floss: red and cream
- Embroidery needle

Finished quilt: 10×12½"

Yardages and cutting instructions are based on 52"-wide felted wool and 42" of usable cotton fabric width.

cut fabrics

Cut pieces in the following order. Patterns are on *pages 34* and *35*.

To felt your own wool, machine-wash it in a hot-water-wash, cool-rinse cycle. Machine-dry it on high heat and steam-press.

To use freezer paper to cut appliqué shapes, complete the following steps.

1. Lay freezer paper, shiny side down, over patterns. With a pencil, trace each pattern the number of times indicated in cutting instructions, leaving ¼" between tracings. Cut out freezer-paper shapes roughly ⅛" outside traced lines.

2. Using a hot dry iron, press freezer-paper shapes, shiny sides down, onto cream wool; let cool. Cut out wool shapes on drawn lines. Peel off freezer paper.

From cream wool, cut:

- 1—10½×13" rectangle for appliqué foundation
- 1 *each* of patterns A, B, C, D, E, F, G, H, I, K, L, and M
- 9 of Pattern J
- 2 *each* of patterns N, O, and P
- 4 *each* of patterns Q and Q reversed
- 1 *each* of letters w, l, c, o, and m
- 2 of letter e

From red stripe, cut:

- 3—2½×21" binding strips

appliqué and embroider quilt top

Refer to Basic Stitches, beginning on *page 154*, for blanket stitch, running stitch, chain stitch, lazy daisy stitch, and French knot instructions. Use two strands of red embroidery floss for all stitches.

1. Referring to **Appliqué Placement Diagram,** *page 32*, position A cottage, B roof, C chimney, D and E smoke, F door frame, and G, H, and I window frames on cream wool 10½×13" appliqué foundation; baste in place.

2. Blanket-stitch around edges of each piece, working from bottom layer to top. Note: Designer Janet Carija Brandt stitched both long and short blanket stitches along the top edge of the B roof. The ends of the blanket stitches on each side of the G, H, and I window frames meet in the middle to create the appearance of continuous lines.

3 Use running stitches to make shingles on the cottage and boards on the door.

4 Referring to photo, *opposite*, chain-stitch the lower edge of the B roof, inside the window frames, on the door, and between the door and the door frame.

5 Make three lazy daisy stitches at the center of the roof.

6 Referring to **Appliqué Placement Diagram** and photo, arrange remaining appliqué pieces on appliqué foundation; baste. Note: The right arm of the K bear folds to show on top of the Q reversed fence rail. The Q and Q reversed fence rails weave under and over the L, M, N, O, and P fence posts and are trimmed after appliquéing is complete.

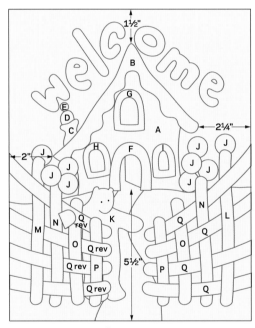

APPLIQUÉ PLACEMENT DIAGRAM

7 Blanket-stitch around the edges of each Step 6 piece, working from the bottom layer to the top. Trim the Q and Q reversed fence rails even with the edges of the appliqué foundation.

8 Chain-stitch a single row through the center of each letter, double rows from the cottage's lower outer corners to the edges of the appliqué foundation, a single row along bottom edge of cottage, double rows to make the path's edges, and triple rows through the center of each fence rail and fence post.

9 Make lazy daisy stitches at the center of each J flower.

10 Add French knots for the bear's eyes.

11 Blanket-stitch cobblestones for the path between the rows of chain stitches to make the appliquéd foundation. Start at the doorway and work toward the fence; overlap each new row of stitches with the previous row, pulling slightly to create a honeycomb effect (**Overlapping Blanket Stitch Diagram**).

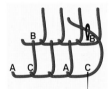

OVERLAPPING BLANKET STITCH DIAGRAM

12 Add a French knot at center of each cobblestone.

13 Trim appliquéd foundation to 10×12½" including seam allowances to complete the quilt top.

finish quilt

1 Layer quilt top, batting, and backing; baste. (For details, see Finishing, *page 159*.)

2 Quilt as desired. This project was hand-stitched using cream embroidery floss to quilt a line of running stitches every ½" across the house for siding and around the edge of the quilt.

3 Bind with red stripe binding strips. (For details, see Finishing.)

 If you wish to use wool from a piece of clothing for a project, cut it apart and remove the seams before felting so the wool can shrink freely.

Welcome
Cottage
Pattern B

E

Pattern D

Pattern C

Welcome Cottage
Pattern A

Pattern
M

Pattern
L

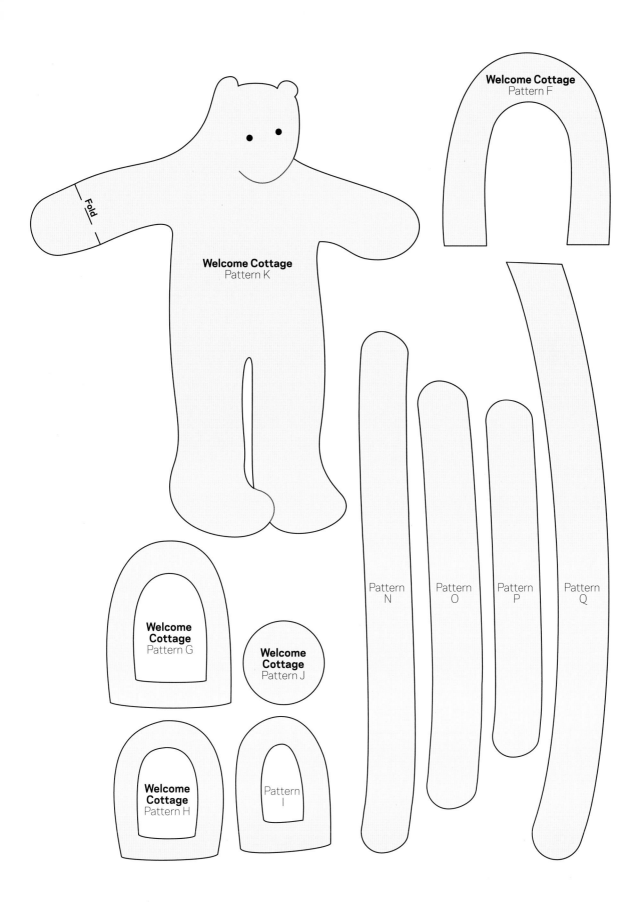

Welcome Cottage
Pattern F

Welcome Cottage
Pattern K

Fold

Pattern
N

Pattern
O

Pattern
P

Pattern
Q

Welcome Cottage
Pattern G

Welcome Cottage
Pattern J

Welcome Cottage
Pattern H

Pattern
I

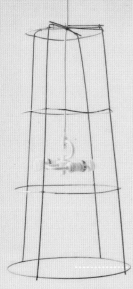

PIECED *together*

Fit a tomato cage with an embroidered slipcover to transform it into a pendant lamp. DESIGNER **JENI WRIGHT**

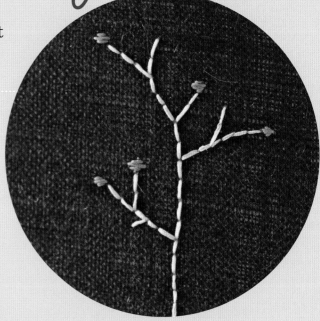

materials

- 1½ to 2 yards fabric (slipcover)
- Wire cutters
- Large tomato cage
- Pendant light kit
- Newspaper
- Tracing paper
- Transfer paper
- Embroidery floss: ecru, orange, black
- Embroidery needle

Yardages and cutting instructions are based on 42" of usable fabric width. **Measurements** include ½" seam allowances. Sew with right sides together unless otherwise stated.

assemble cage unit and slipcover

1. Using wire cutters, cut a large tomato cage down to the desired size of your pendant lamp. Turn upside down.

2. Bend the wires meant to push into the ground over the top of the cage as shown in photo, *above*. String a pendant light kit through the center of the bent-in wires to make a cage unit.

3. To create a newspaper template, roll the cage unit over the paper, creating an arc and tracing as you go. Add 1" to top and bottom edges and cut out the template.

4. Using the template as a guide, cut the slipcover from the fabric. (If desired, machine-stitch two pieces of contrasting fabric together to fit the pattern; see photo *opposite*.) Press under the top and bottom edges ½"; stitch to hem edges.

embroider and finish lamp

Refer to Basic Stitches, beginning on *page 154*, for backstitch, satin stitch, and blanket stitch instructions.

1. Using tracing and transfer paper, transfer the Full-Size Embroidery Pattern on *Pattern Sheet 2* onto the bottom portion of the slipcover, repeating the motif across the fabric width.

2. Backstitch the stems with four strands of ecru embroidery floss (see photo, *above*). Satin-stitch the buds with six strands of orange floss.

3. Sew embroidered slipcover ends together to make a cylinder shape. Slide slipcover over the cage unit. Fold the top and bottom edges under; hand-stitch the fabric to the inside of the cage unit.

4. Blanket-stitch the bottom edge of the slipcover with six strands of black floss to complete the pendant lamp.

A sweet songbird and a classic branch-and-leaf pattern combine
to create a pillow and sheet ensemble that is easy and fun to stitch.
DESIGNER **ALICE OKON**

sweet slumber

Toss Pillow

materials

- Purchased solid green toss pillow with removable cover
- Tracing paper
- Transfer paper
- Perle cotton No. 5: lavender
- Needles: embroidery and beading
- Seed beads: purple

embellish pillow cover

1 Remove the pillow form and lay the pillow cover flat. Using tracing and transfer paper, transfer the Branch Full-Size Embroidery Pattern on *page 41* vertically onto one corner of the pillow cover. Repeat to transfer a second branch, positioning the pattern horizontally in the same corner of the pillow cover.

2 Using lavender perle cotton, stem-stitch along marked lines. (Refer to Basic Stitches, beginning on *page 154*, for stem stitch instructions.) Add a stem-stitched border ¼" from the pillow cover edges (see photo, *above*).

3 Hand-stitch clusters of purple seed beads along the embroidered branches to complete the pillow cover.

Sheet Set

materials

- White flat sheet with lavender cuff
- Two white pillowcases with lavender cuffs
- Air- or water-soluble fabric pen
- Perle cotton No. 5: 3 skeins white, 2 skeins lavender, 2 skeins purple
- Embroidery needle

trace patterns

1 Tape the Branch Full-Size Embroidery Pattern, *page 41*, to a light box or bright window. Find the center point of the flat sheet's lavender cuff and center the cuff atop the pattern. Trace the pattern onto the sheet cuff with the fabric pen. Continue positioning and tracing the branch pattern along the sheet cuff, leaving 2¼" between branches.

2 Repeat Step 1 to trace the branch pattern on each pillowcase cuff.

3 Find the center point of one pillowcase. Place the Bird-and-Branch Full-Size Embroidery Pattern on *Pattern Sheet 1* between the pillowcase layers, centering the pattern. Trace as before. Repeat with the second pillowcase, reversing the bird-and-branch pattern so the bird faces the opposite direction.

embroider sheet and pillowcases

Refer to Basic Stitches, beginning on *page 154*, for backstitch and French knot instructions. Wrap perle cotton around needle two times for a double-wrapped French knot.

1 Backstitch the branches on the sheet and pillowcase cuffs using white perle cotton (see photo, *page 39*).

2 For the bird-and-branch patterns on the pillowcases, use lavender perle cotton to backstitch the branches and leaves, and make a double-wrapped French knot in the center of each bird's eye (see photo, *above*). Backstitch the curved wreath shapes with purple perle cotton. Backstitch each bird body and small feather lines with purple perle cotton, and add double-wrapped French knots to the wings as indicated on the pattern to complete the embroidered sheet and pillowcases.

Sweet Slumber
Branch
Full-Size Embroidery Pattern

tip

Use an embroidery hoop
to secure the fabric while you
embroider. It will hold the
fabric taut, maintain even
tension for your stitches,
and keep the fabric cleaner.

before AND after

Embroidery on surfaces
other than fabric? Yes! Think
outside of the box with big
stitches on thrift store finds.
DESIGNER **JENI WRIGHT**

before

before

OPPOSITE: Open a new chapter in an old wooden crate's life with whimsical dandelion stitching (drill the design first to accommodate the stitching). Different types of yarn yield unique results (fuzzy for flowers, smooth for stems). **THIS PAGE:** Create an enchanting wall display from a collection of discount store wooden serving trays by spray-painting them in vibrant hues, then embroidering each with fun imagery.

Paint a super-size greeting and stitch a large-scale flower on an old cabinet. This flea market find was base-coated white, masked off with contact-paper letters, then painted gray-green and embellished with a stitched allium flower.

before

2. Using a drill with ¹⁄₁₆" drill bit, carefully drill a pilot hole where each dot is located on the pattern. After all the holes are drilled, change to a ³⁄₁₆" drill bit and enlarge the center dandelion hole at top of stem. Change to a ¹⁄₈" drill bit and enlarge the center hole of each seed head. Change to a ³⁄₃₂" drill bit and enlarge the outer holes of each seed head. Remove all wood dust.

embroider crate

Refer to Basic Stitches, beginning on *page 154,* for backstitch, straight stitch, and French knot instructions. Wrap yarn around needle one time for a single-wrapped French knot. Use one strand of yarn or twine for all embroidery. Secure yarn and twine ends to the inside of the crate using a staple gun.

1. Using a yarn needle, backstitch the dandelion stem with green yarn by stitching through the holes.

2. Straight-stitch the dandelion spokes with cream twine, working the stitches from the outside and bringing each stitch back through the large center hole at the top of the stem.

3. Straight-stitch each seed head with white yarn, working the stitches from the outer holes and bringing each stitch back through the seed head center hole.

4. Add a single-wrapped French knot with yellow yarn to each seed head center hole to complete the crate.

Wooden Crate

(shown *above* and on *page 42*)

materials

- Wooden crate
- Tracing paper
- Transfer paper
- Drill
- Drill bits: ¹⁄₁₆", ³⁄₃₂", ¹⁄₈", and ³⁄₁₆"
- Staple gun
- Yarn: green, white, yellow
- Twine: cream
- Yarn needle

prepare crate

1. Trace the Wooden Crate Full-Size Embroidery Pattern on *Pattern Sheet 3* onto tracing paper. Lay the crate with the side you want to embellish facing up. Lay transfer paper on the crate, then position the traced design on top of the transfer paper. Trace the design again using a stylus or ball-point pen, pressing firmly so the pattern transfers onto the wood.

 tip ▷ Small-scale motifs, such as those shown on *page 43,* are a great way to use leftover yarn or ribbon. Try thin ribbon for the flowers or French knots to enhance the texture.

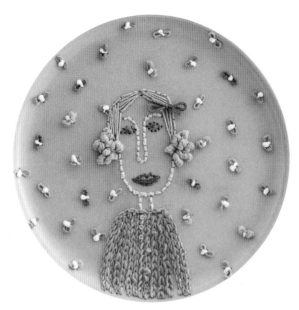

embroider plate

Refer to Basic Stitches, beginning on *page 154*, for backstitch, straight stitch, chain stitch, and French knot instructions. Wrap yarn around needle one time for a single-wrapped French knot, and three times for a triple-wrapped French knot. Use one strand of yarn for all embroidery.

1. Using a yarn needle, backstitch the outline of the face, neck, nose, and eyebrows with ivory yarn (see photo, *left*).

2. Straight-stitch the hair with yellow yarn. Add triple-wrapped French knots along the sides of the face using yellow yarn.

3. Chain-stitch the shirt with orange yarn, working the stitches from the neckline to the edge of the plate.

4. Backstitch the lips with pink yarn.

5. Backstitch the outline for each eye with tan yarn. Add a single-wrapped French knot with lavender yarn for each pupil.

6. Sew three yellow buttons to the top of the chain-stitched shirt. Tie a bow onto the hair with lavender yarn.

7. Loop a length of light or medium green yarn through each remaining hole. Using white yarn, secure the center of each loop with a single-wrapped French knot to complete the plate.

Girl Plate
materials

- Round wooden plate, at least 8" diameter
- Spray paint: pink
- Tracing paper
- Transfer paper
- Drill
- Drill bits: $\frac{1}{16}$" and $\frac{3}{32}$"
- Yarn: ivory, yellow, orange, pink, tan, lavender, light green, medium green, white
- Yarn needle
- Three small buttons: yellow

prepare plate

1. Spray-paint the plate with pink paint; allow to dry.

2. Trace the Girl Plate Full-Size Embroidery Pattern on *Pattern Sheet 3* onto tracing paper. Lay transfer paper on the plate, then position the traced design on top of the transfer paper. Trace the design again using a stylus or ball-point pen, pressing firmly so the pattern transfers onto the plate.

3. Using a drill with $\frac{1}{16}$" drill bit, carefully drill a pilot hole where each dot is located on the pattern. After all the holes are drilled, change to a $\frac{3}{32}$" drill bit and enlarge the shirt holes and the hair holes on the sides of the face. Drill random holes in the space surrounding the girl. Remove all wood dust.

tip

Make your own custom stencils by enlarging words or graphics on a computer, tracing the designs onto contact paper, and cutting them out.

Butterfly Plate

materials

- Round wooden plate, at least 8" diameter
- Plate that is approximately 2" in diameter smaller than wooden plate
- Contact paper
- Spray paint: blue
- Tracing paper
- Transfer paper
- Drill
- Drill bit: 1/16"
- Yarn: pink, orange, brown, red, lavender, teal
- Yarn needle

prepare plate

1. Lay the wooden plate facedown on contact paper and trace around it using a pencil. Lay a second smaller plate facedown in the center and trace around it. Cut out both circles, discarding the center circle. Press the contact-paper ring that remains around the rim of the wooden plate to act as a mask. Spray-paint the plate center with blue paint; allow to dry. Remove the contact-paper mask to reveal a crisp painted edge.

2. Trace the Butterfly Plate Full-Size Embroidery Pattern on *Pattern Sheet 3* onto tracing paper. Lay transfer paper on the plate, then position the traced design on top of the transfer paper. Trace the design again using a stylus or ball-point pen, pressing firmly so the pattern transfers onto the plate.

3. Using a pencil and a ruler, evenly mark dots that are approximately 1" apart along the circular painted edge.

4. Using a drill with a 1/16" drill bit, carefully drill a hole where each dot is located on the pattern and circular edge. Remove all wood dust.

embroider plate

Refer to Basic Stitches, beginning on *page 154*, for backstitch, satin stitch, straight stitch, and French knot instructions. Wrap yarn around needle two times for a double-wrapped French knot and three times for a triple-wrapped French knot. Use one strand of yarn for all embroidery.

1. Using yarn needle, backstitch upper wings of butterfly with pink yarn (see photo, *left*). Backstitch lower wings with orange yarn.

2. Using brown yarn, satin-stitch the butterfly body and straight-stitch the antennae. Add triple-wrapped French knots to the antennae with brown yarn.

3. Backstitch the outlines for the spots on the lower wings with red yarn. Straight-stitch the spot centers with pink yarn.

4. Add a row of double-wrapped French knots to each upper wing using red yarn. With orange yarn, add a row of triple-wrapped French knots below the red knots on each upper wing.

5. Add a row of double-wrapped French knots to each lower wing using lavender yarn. With red yarn, add one triple-wrapped French knot to each lower wing.

6. Using teal yarn, create a woven, framed effect around the painted edge of the plate. First bring the yarn up through a hole, then push the needle down through a hole across the plate to create a 1"-wide border. Extend yarn across back of plate, bringing the needle up next to the first hole. Continue to work in one direction around plate. When you reach the starting point, reverse direction and work back around the plate until you reach the first hole again to complete the plate.

Spotted Flower Plate

materials
- 8"-square wooden plate with rim
- Tracing paper
- Contact paper
- Spray paint: teal and lime green
- Transfer paper
- Drill
- Drill bits: $\frac{1}{16}$" and $\frac{3}{32}$"
- Yarn: red, white, yellow
- Yarn needle

prepare plate

1. Trace only the square polka-dot portion of the Spotted Flower Plate Full-Size Embroidery Pattern on *Pattern Sheet 3* onto tracing paper. Using a light box or bright window, trace the design onto contact paper. Cut out the square and each circle to make a mask.

2. Press the square contact paper portion of the mask onto the center of the plate. Replace the contact-paper circles. Carefully peel away the square portion, leaving just the circles behind. Spray-paint the center of the plate with teal paint; allow to dry. Peel off the contact-paper circles.

3. Cut a 5¾" square from contact paper. Press the contact-paper square over the painted center of the plate. Spray-paint the rim of the plate with lime green paint; allow to dry. Peel off the square mask.

4. Again using the pattern on *Pattern Sheet 3*, trace the flower pattern and square outline with dots onto tracing paper (you do not need to trace the large polka dots). Lay transfer paper on the plate, then position the traced design atop the transfer paper. Trace the design again using a stylus or ball-point pen, pressing firmly so pattern transfers onto the plate.

5. Using a drill with a $\frac{1}{16}$" drill bit, carefully drill a hole where each dot is located on the pattern. After all the holes are drilled, change to a $\frac{3}{32}$" drill bit and enlarge the holes in the center of the flower. Remove all wood dust.

embroider plate

Refer to Basic Stitches, beginning on *page 154*, for running stitch, lazy daisy stitch, and French knot instructions. Wrap yarn around needle four times for a quadruple-wrapped French knot. Use one strand of yarn for all embroidery.

1. Using a yarn needle and red yarn, make running stitches to outline the center of the plate (see photo, *above left*).

2. Make loose lazy daisy stitches with white yarn for flower petals.

3. Using yellow yarn, add quadruple-wrapped French knots to the flower center to complete the plate.

tip Contact paper works great for masking off areas where you want the wood tones of the plate to show through after painting.

Letter Plate

materials

- Small wooden plate
- Spray paint: hot pink
- Contact paper
- Drill
- Drill bit: 1/16"
- Yarn: blue
- Yarn needle

prepare plate

1. Spray-paint the plate with hot pink paint; allow to dry.

2. Using a computer, type and print the desired monogram letter in a simple font. Enlarge the letter as desired to fit your plate.

3. Cut a piece of contact paper slightly larger than the letter. Lay the contact paper over the letter and trace around the letter with a pencil. Cut out the contact-paper letter.

4. Press the contact-paper letter onto the plate.

5. Using a drill with a 1/16" drill bit, carefully drill holes randomly around the edges of the letter. Remove all wood dust.

embroider plate

Refer to Basic Stitches, beginning on *page 154*, for French knot instructions. Wrap yarn around needle two times for a double-wrapped French knot and three times for a triple-wrapped French knot. Use one strand of yarn for all embroidery.

1. Using a yarn needle and blue yarn, stitch a double-wrapped or triple-wrapped French knot through each hole (see photo, *left*).

2. Remove the contact-paper letter to complete the plate.

Branch Tray

materials

- Oblong wooden tray
- Tracing paper
- Contact paper
- Crafts knife
- Spray paint: teal
- Transfer paper
- Drill
- Drill bits: 1/16" and 3/32"
- Yarn: light green, dark green, hot pink, red
- Yarn needle

prepare tray

1. Trace the branch portion of the Branch Tray Full-Size Embroidery Pattern on *Pattern Sheet 3* onto tracing paper (do not trace cherries and leaves). Using a light box or bright window, trace branch onto contact paper. Cut out the design using a crafts knife to make a branch mask.

2. Press the contact-paper branch mask onto the tray. Spray-paint the tray with teal paint; allow to dry. Peel off the mask.

3. Again using the pattern on *Pattern Sheet 3*, trace cherries and leaves with dots onto tracing paper (you do not need to trace the branch). Lay transfer paper on the tray, then position traced design atop the transfer paper. Trace the design again using a stylus or ball-point pen, pressing firmly so the pattern transfers onto tray.

4 Using a drill with a 1/16" drill bit, carefully drill the holes for the leaves and stems. Change to a 3/32" drill bit and drill the cherry holes. Remove all wood dust.

embroider tray

Refer to Basic Stitches, beginning on *page 154*, for backstitch and French knot instructions. Wrap yarn around needle three times for a triple-wrapped French knot. Use one strand of yarn for all embroidery.

1 Backstitch the leaf outlines and stems with light green yarn (see photo, *page 49*). Backstitch the leaf centers with dark green yarn.

2 Add triple-wrapped French knots for the cherries, using hot pink yarn for the top of each cherry and red yarn for the bottom of each cherry, to complete the tray.

Cabinet

(shown *below right* and on *page 44*)

materials

- Wooden cabinet
- Medium- and fine-grit sandpaper
- Tack cloth
- Glossy latex paint in desired colors for letters and cabinet body
- Wide paintbrush
- Contact paper
- Crafts knife
- Transfer paper
- Drill
- Drill bit: 3/16"
- Staple gun
- Yarn: olive green and blue
- Wool roving: blue
- Yarn needle

prepare cabinet

1 Sand the cabinet with sandpaper using medium-grit, then fine-grit sandpaper. Remove the sanding dust with a tack cloth.

2 Base-coat the cabinet using the paint color desired for the letters. Allow to dry.

3 Using a computer, type and print the desired words (see photo, *page 44*). Enlarge words to the desired size. Trace the words onto contact paper and cut out the letters using a crafts knife to make letter masks.

4 Press the letter masks onto the cabinet in desired positions, wrapping them around the edges of the cabinet if desired. Top-coat the cabinet using the paint color desired for the cabinet body. When the paint is dry, peel off the letter masks.

5 Enlarge the Cabinet Embroidery Pattern from *Pattern Sheet 3* using a photocopier to achieve the desired size. Position transfer paper on the cabinet front, then lay the enlarged paper pattern atop the transfer paper. Trace the design using a stylus or ball-point pen, pressing firmly so the pattern transfers onto the wood.

6 Using a drill with a 3/16" drill bit, carefully drill a hole where each dot is located on the pattern. Remove all wood dust.

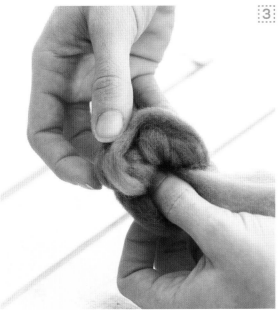

embroider cabinet

Refer to Basic Stitches, beginning on *page 154*, for backstitch instructions. Use two strands of yarn for the embroidery. Secure yarn ends to the inside of the cabinet doors using a staple gun.

1. Using a yarn needle, backstitch the stem and flower head with olive green yarn by stitching through the holes.

2. Peel off a 1"-thick section of blue wool roving from the bundle and gently twist the wool (**Photo 1**).

3. Tie the twisted wool into a pretzel shape—the looser, the better (**Photo 2**).

4. Feed the ends of the wool through the center of the knot to create a loose flower (**photos 3** and **4**). Using blue yarn, secure the ends on the back with loose tack stitches. Attach the flower to a hole drilled in the cabinet, tacking it in place with blue yarn.

5. Repeat steps 2–4 to attach the remaining flowers and complete the cabinet.

HERE'S THE *key*

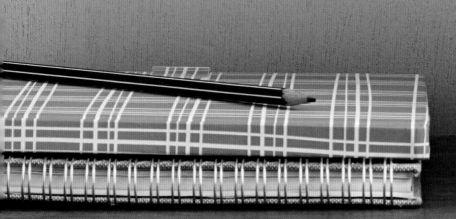

Unlock your cross-stitch skills and open the door to creativity by stitching brightly colored skeleton keys and hanging them up in a wooden embroidery hoop. DESIGNER **TINA FITZPATRICK**

materials

- 10"-square 14-count white Aida cloth
- 6"-diameter wooden embroidery hoop
- Embroidery floss: aqua, red, green
- Tapestry needle, size 24

Finished project: 6" diameter

embroider and finish design

Refer to Basic Stitches, beginning on *page 154,* for cross-stitch instructions. Use three strands of embroidery floss to make cross-stitches over one square of the fabric.

1. Fold white Aida cloth square in half horizontally and vertically to find center; press lightly and unfold.

2. Place Aida cloth in embroidery hoop if desired, centering the fabric. Pull fabric taut; tighten the screw.

3. Referring to Cross-Stitch Pattern and Color Key, *below,* use aqua, red, and green floss to cross-stitch the keys.

4. Remove fabric from the embroidery hoop. Refer to Finishing, beginning on *page 159,* for blocking instructions. Insert fabric into the hoop, centering the design and pulling fabric taut. Trim excess fabric on the back side of the hoop to complete the project.

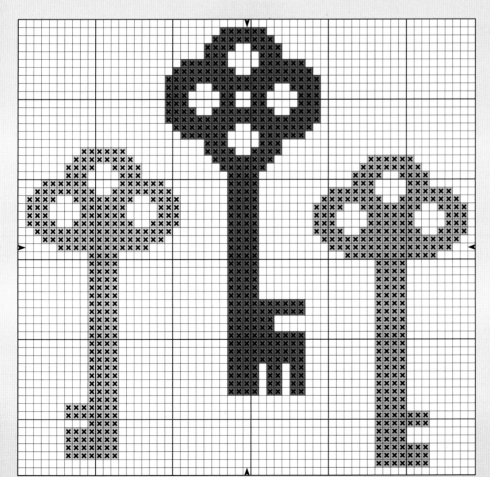

COLOR KEY
- ☒ Aqua
- ☒ Red
- ☒ Green

Here's the Key
Cross-Stitch Pattern

1 Square = 1 Stitch

HOLIDAY

There's something about holiday embroidery that evokes the nostalgia of yesteryear. Bring magic to your festive decorating with these charming seasonal designs.

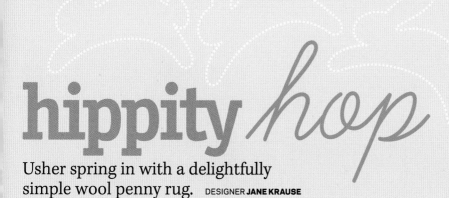

hippity *hop*

Usher spring in with a delightfully
simple wool penny rug. DESIGNER **JANE KRAUSE**

materials
- 14×16" rectangle cream felted wool
  (appliqué foundation, pennies, center unit)
- 12" square tan felted wool (rabbit appliqué,
  pennies)
- Scraps of purple, yellow, pink, green,
  light blue, and blue felted wools (flower
  appliqués, pennies)
- Freezer paper
- Embroidery floss: tan, yellow, pink, green,
  purple, light blue, blue
- Embroidery needle

Finished penny rug: 10×8"

cut fabrics
Cut pieces in the following order. Patterns are
on *Pattern Sheet 4*.

To felt your own wool, machine-wash it in a
hot-water wash, cool-rinse cycle. Machine-dry
it on high heat and steam-press.

To use freezer paper to cut wool shapes,
complete the following steps.

1 Lay freezer paper, shiny side down, over
patterns. Use a pencil to trace each
pattern the number of times indicated in
cutting instructions, leaving ¼" between
tracings. Cut out freezer-paper shapes
roughly ⅛" outside traced lines.

2 Using a hot dry iron, press each freezer-
paper shape, shiny side down, onto
designated wool; let cool. Cut out wool
shapes on drawn lines. Peel off
freezer paper.

From cream wool, cut:
- 2 of Pattern A
- 18 of Pattern E

From tan wool, cut:
- 1 of Pattern B
- 18 of Pattern E

From purple wool, cut:
- 1 of Pattern C

From yellow wool, cut:
- 1 of Pattern D

**From assorted purple, yellow, pink, green,
light blue, and blue wools, cut:**
- 18 of Pattern F

appliqué and embroider center unit

Refer to Basic Stitches, beginning on *page 154*, for whipstitch, French knot, running stitch, straight stitch, and blanket stitch instructions.

1. Referring to photo, *page 56*, position the tan wool B bunny, purple wool C circle, and yellow wool D circle on a cream wool A oval. Baste pieces in place.

To adapt a wool appliqué project to a traditional hand-appliqué one, be certain to add a ³⁄₁₆" seam allowance to the edges of each shape.

2. Using one strand of tan embroidery floss, whipstitch around the bunny shape.

3. Using two strands of yellow floss, make a French knot in the flower center, stitching through all layers. With two strands of pink floss, make a French knot for the bunny's eye.

4. Using five strands of tan floss, make a single running stitch at the tip of the bunny's nose; stitch through all layers and begin and end the stitch on the top side, leaving 3" tails. Tie the tails in a square knot on the surface of the cream wool oval. Trim the thread tails to ³⁄₁₆" to form whiskers.

5. Using two strands of green floss, make straight stitches for the flower stem, leaves, and grass.

Designer Notes

The pieces in Jane Krause's penny rug were die-cut with an Accu-Cut system. "Everything is cut precisely, so there are no rough or uneven edges," she says.

Jane prefers a primitive look, and she likes to work with hand-dyed, felted wools such as those in this penny rug. However, she finds this a very versatile project.

"You could make it in paper, for cards," she says. "Or trace the patterns in flannel, brushed cottons, or cotton, in addition to wool."

6 Referring to the photo, *opposite*, center an assorted wool F circle atop a cream or tan wool E circle. Using three strands of floss to match the F circle, make a star stitch through all layers to make an appliquéd penny.

To make a star stitch, pull the needle up at A, then push it down at B (**Star Stitch Diagram**). Bring the needle up at C and again push the needle down at B. Pull the needle up at D and again push it down at B. Continue in the same manner around the F circle to make a star stitch.

STAR STITCH DIAGRAM

7 Repeat Step 6 to make 18 appliquéd pennies total (nine pennies with cream E pieces and nine pennies with tan E pieces).

8 Using three strands of tan floss, blanket-stitch each appliquéd penny to a matching-color E circle. Blanket-stitch the remaining cream A oval to the wrong side of the appliquéd cream A oval to make the center unit.

finish penny rug

1 Using one strand of tan floss, slip-stitch the pennies to the outer edge of the center unit and to one another.

2 Use six strands of purple floss to make a small bow. Tack the bow in place at the bunny's neck to complete the penny rug.

HALLOWEEN
queen

This enchanting pumpkin lady lights the way with
wool appliqués and a medley of embroidery stitches.

DESIGNER **JANET CARIJA BRANDT**

materials
- 8¼×22" piece orange felted wool (appliqué foundation, appliqués)
- ½ yard solid orange (backing, binding)
- 11×13" lightweight batting
- Freezer paper
- Embroidery floss: black
- Embroidery needle

Finished quilt: 8¼×10¼"

cut fabrics
Cut pieces in the following order. Patterns are on *pages 62* and *63*.

To felt your own wool, machine-wash it in a hot-water-wash, cool-rinse cycle. Machine-dry it on high heat and steam-press.

To use freezer paper to cut appliqué shapes, complete the following steps.

1. Lay freezer paper, shiny side down, over patterns. With a pencil, trace each pattern the number of times indicated in cutting instructions, leaving ¼" between tracings. Cut out freezer-paper shapes roughly ⅛" outside traced lines.

2. Using a hot dry iron, press freezer-paper shapes, shiny sides down, onto orange wool; let cool. Cut out wool shapes on drawn lines. Peel off freezer paper.

From orange wool, cut:
- 1—8¼×10¼" rectangle for appliqué foundation
- 1 *each* of patterns A, B, C, D, E, F, G, H, I, J, K, L, M, N, O, P, and Q
- 2 of Pattern R

From solid orange, cut:
- 3—2½×21" binding strips
- 1—11×13" rectangle for backing

appliqué and embroider quilt top
Refer to Basic Stitches, beginning on *page 154*, for blanket stitch, chain stitch, and French knot instructions. Wrap floss around needle two times for a double-wrapped French knot. Use two strands of black embroidery floss for all stitches.

1. Referring to **Appliqué Placement Diagram**, position and baste all appliqué shapes atop orange wool 8¼×10¼" appliqué foundation. Blanket-stitch each piece in place.

APPLIQUÉ PLACEMENT DIAGRAM

2. Referring to photo, *page 60*, use chain stitches to create the pumpkin stems around the head, to fill in the eyes and mouth, to add stripes to the collar and the skirt ruffle, to make lighting accents around the lantern, to fill in the lantern, and to add the apron and skirt lines.

3. Add double-wrapped French knots to the skirt ruffle.

4. Decorate the skirt with blanket stitches to complete the quilt top; overlap each new row of stitches with the previous row, pulling slightly to create a honeycomb effect (**Overlapping Blanket Stitch Diagram**).

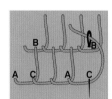

OVERLAPPING BLANKET STITCH DIAGRAM

finish quilt

1. Layer quilt top, batting, and backing; baste. (For details, see Finishing, *page 159*.) Quilt as desired.

2. Bind with solid orange binding strips. (For details, see Finishing.)

Halloween Queen Pattern O

Halloween Queen Pattern M

Halloween Queen Pattern P

Halloween Queen Pattern N

Halloween Queen Pattern Q

Halloween Queen Pattern R

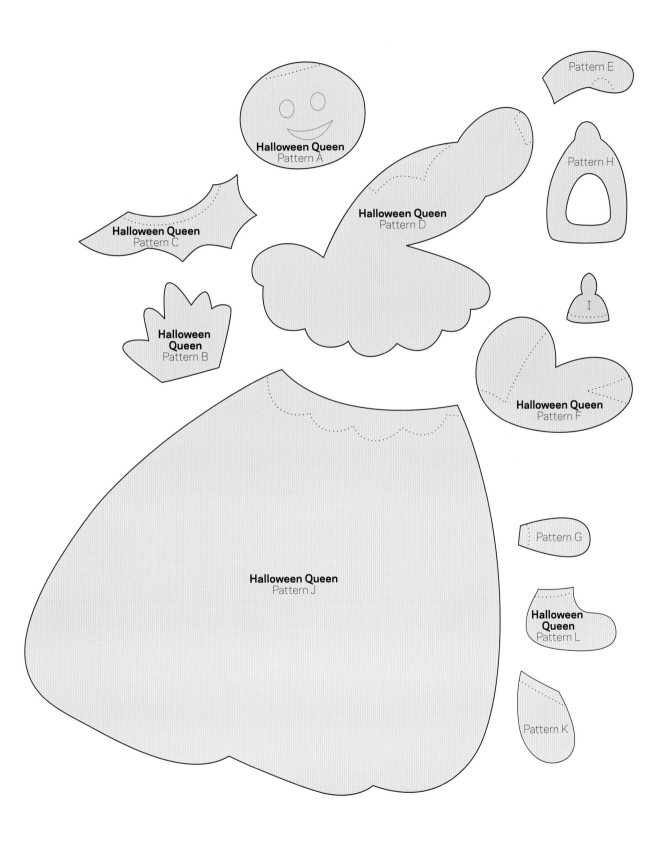

Halloween Queen
Pattern A

Halloween Queen
Pattern C

Halloween
Queen
Pattern B

Halloween Queen
Pattern D

Pattern E

Pattern H

I

Halloween Queen
Pattern F

Halloween Queen
Pattern J

Pattern G

Halloween
Queen
Pattern L

Pattern K

halloween FRIENDS

Embroider one or both of these fun Halloween designs onto infant bodysuits or a kid's T-shirt to scare up a fun time. DESIGNER **HEIDI PALKOVIC**

materials
for two bodysuits

- Two solid white infant bodysuits
- Lightweight fusible stabilizer
- Air- or water-soluble fabric pen
- Embroidery floss: fluorescent orange, black, fluorescent pink, fluorescent purple, fluorescent blue
- Embroidery needle

embroider bodysuits

Refer to Basic Stitches, beginning on *page 154*, for backstitch, French knot, satin stitch, and straight stitch instructions. Wrap floss around needle two times for a double-wrapped French knot. Use three strands of embroidery floss for all stitches.

1. Using the Baby Girl and Baby Boy Full-Size Embroidery patterns, *below*, and a light box or bright window, trace one design onto each bodysuit with fabric pen.

2. Cut two pieces of stabilizer that are slightly larger than the embroidery patterns. Following manufacturer's instructions, fuse stabilizer onto back of each traced design.

3. For the "Ghoul-friend" baby girl bodysuit, backstitch the lettering with fluorescent orange floss. Using black floss, backstitch the ghost and bow outline, add a backstitch smile, and make double-wrapped French knots for the eyes. Fill in the bow using fluorescent pink floss and satin stitches.

4. For the "Boo-friend" baby boy bodysuit, backstitch the lettering with fluorescent purple floss. Using black floss, backstitch the cat and collar outlines, and add small straight stitches for the eyes. Fill in the collar using fluorescent blue floss and double-wrapped French knots.

Halloween Friends
Baby Girl Full-Size Embroidery Pattern

Halloween Friends
Baby Boy Full-Size Embroidery Pattern

pumpkin perfect

This lovely needle-punch design, featuring an embroidered wool mat and star button, will look stunning on a wall or mantel all autumn long.

materials

- 11" square weaver's cloth (needle-punch foundation)
- 8" square burnt orange felted wool (mat)
- Fine-point permanent marker
- 1⅛"-diameter star button
- 7"-diameter locking embroidery hoop
- Three skeins *each* of ecru and black embroidery floss
- 3-strand punch needle
- Fabric pen
- Black frame with 6"-square back opening and mounting board
- Embroidery needle
- Fabric glue (optional)

Finished design: 6" square (excluding frame)

prepare foundation

1. Tape the Full-Size Needle-Punch Pattern, *page 69*, to a light box or bright window. Center and tape the weaver's cloth 11" square over the pattern so the fabric stretches from top to bottom.

2. Use the permanent marker to trace the solid pattern lines onto the fabric. Using dashed lines as a guide, position the star button on the fabric with right side down; trace the shape onto the fabric with the marker to make a needle-punch foundation. (The traced lines are on the back side of the design.)

needle-punch design

1. With traced pattern side up, tightly secure the needle-punch foundation in the locking hoop without distorting the design.

2. Separate the strands of ecru and black embroidery floss; thread the punch needle following the manufacturer's instructions.

3. For this design, the needle indicator pin, which controls the height of the loops on the front, was set to 1. Use the shortest needle length that you feel comfortable with to punch the design.

4. To begin, use black floss to outline the pumpkin with needle-punch stitches just inside the outer shape line. Make the stitches very close together so no space shows between them. To ensure a perfect fit for the button, punch directly on the lines for the star. Fill in the pumpkin with black floss; do not punch inside the star shape.

5. Continue with black floss, punching directly on the lines for the pumpkin vine and the scalloped inner border. In addition, punch directly on the outer border line and then again just beyond it to create a border that is two punch stitches wide.

6 Using ecru floss, start stitching the background by outlining each of the previously punched elements. Continue adding consecutive rows of punches just beyond these outlines until the outlines meet. Fill in any remaining spaces to complete the background.

7 Trim any long or loose pieces of floss, including beginning and ending thread tails, to the same length as the punched loops. Snuggle the button into the unpunched star space; use matching thread to hand-sew the button in place.

prepare mat

To felt your own wool, machine-wash it in a hot-water-wash, cool-rinse cycle. Machine-dry it on high heat and steam-press.

Refer to Basic Stitches, beginning on *page 154,* for blanket stitch instructions.

1 Measure the finished punched design. Using a fabric pen, center and draw these measurements onto the burnt orange wool 8" square. Cut along the drawn lines to make a mat.

2 Using an embroidery needle and three strands of black embroidery floss, blanket-stitch along edges of mat opening.

frame design

1 Stretch and mount the punched design on the mounting board. Place the mat atop mounted design so blanket stitches along the mat opening are up against the design's outer punched loops. If desired, apply dots of fabric glue to wrong side of mat to hold it in place. (Take care not to saturate the wool with glue, or it will show on the front.)

2 Trim the mat even with the edges of the mounting board. Place in frame to complete the project.

Supplies

A Weaver's cloth
B Burnt orange felted wool
C Embroidery floss
D Scissors
E 3-strand punch needle
F Star button
G Embroidery needle
H Thread with needle
I Locking embroidery hoop

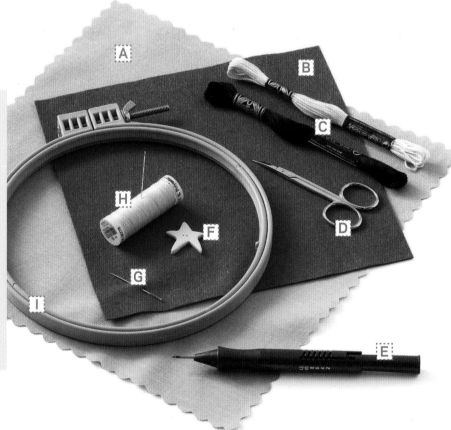

tip

Finish this pumpkin with or without a button. If desired, you can fill the star outline with ecru stitches instead of a button.

Black

Black

Ecru

Black

Pumpkin Perfect
Full-Size Needle-Punch Pattern

banner *holiday*

You know it's a red-letter day when this banner goes on display.
Flagged with peppermint-stripe letters and holiday greenery,
it's sheer joy to embroider and a breeze to finish.   DESIGNER **CRABAPPLE HILL STUDIO**

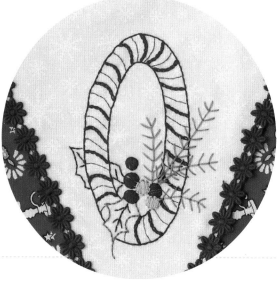

materials
- 12×24" rectangle cream-and-white print (embroidery foundation)
- 2—⅜-yard pieces assorted red prints (background units)
- Air- or water-soluble fabric pen
- 12×24" piece lightweight fusible interfacing
- Embroidery floss: red, blue-green, dark pink, dark green, medium green, golden brown, yellow-green
- Embroidery needle
- 1¼ yards lightweight fusible web
- Pinking shears
- 3 yards ½"-wide flower trim: red
- 1¼ yards satin cord: red

Finished banner:
Approx. 11¼×31½" (excluding cord)

tip

If your Christmas decor isn't red and green, experiment with different floss and fabric colors to coordinate with your holiday scheme.

prepare foundation
1. Tape the Full-Size Embroidery patterns J, O, and Y on *Pattern Sheet 4* to a light box or bright window. Layer cream-and-white print 12×24" rectangle atop patterns. (You will embroider all three letters on a single piece of fabric.) Trace the patterns, including the triangle outlines, onto the fabric using an air- or water-soluble fabric pen.

2. Following manufacturer's instructions, fuse lightweight interfacing 12×24" rectangle to wrong side of traced cream-and-white print rectangle to make the embroidery foundation.

embroider triangles
Refer to Basic Stitches, beginning on *page 154*, for backstitch, chain stitch, French knot, straight stitch, and satin stitch instructions. Use two strands of embroidery floss for all stitches.

1. Referring to the Full-Size Embroidery patterns J, O, and Y; the Stitch Key; and the Color Key on *Pattern Sheet 4* for stitch placement and floss colors, embroider each design as indicated.

2. When stitching is complete, cut out each embroidered triangle on outer traced lines.

assemble pennants

1. Following fusible web manufacturer's directions, fuse the two assorted red print pieces with wrong sides together.

2. The Back Triangle Pattern is on *Pattern Sheet 4*. To make a template, trace the pattern on paper and cut it out. Trace the template three times on one side of the fused red prints. Using pinking shears, cut out each triangle just inside the traced lines to make three background units.

3. Position each J, O, and Y embroidered triangle on a background unit, leaving a ½" border at top edge. Baste each triangle in place to make three pennants.

finish banner

1. Referring to photo on *pages 70* and *71*, cut and baste lengths of red flower trim to pennants, covering edges of embroidered triangles. Leave 2" tails extending from side trim pieces at the top of each triangle.

2. Turn 2" tails under and tack-stitch to wrong sides of pennants to form hanging loops. Machine-stitch trim pieces in place.

3. Thread the red satin cord through the pennant hanging loops to complete the banner.

elfin STOCKINGS

You've made stockings for Santa to fill, but why stop there? Hang this pair on your wall purely for decoration. Stitch the impish designs in embroidered redwork in a weekend. DESIGNER **HILLARY LANG**

materials
for one stocking

- 18×24" rectangle antique white linen (stocking front)
- ⅛ yard red-and-white plaid (cuff units, hanging loop)
- ⅔ yard solid white (stocking back, lining)
- 1¾ yards lightweight fusible interfacing
- Air- or water-soluble fabric pen
- Embroidery floss: red
- Embroidery needle

Finished stocking: 10×19½"

Yardages and cutting instructions are based on 42" of usable fabric width. Measurements include ½" seam allowances unless otherwise indicated. Sew with right sides together unless otherwise stated.

cut fabrics

Cut pieces in the following order.

The Cuff, Stocking, and Lining patterns are on *Pattern Sheet 2*. To make paper templates, trace each pattern on paper and cut out. Pin patterns to fabrics indicated in cutting instructions and cut around the edges. For the cuff template, add ½" seam allowance to bottom edge (dotted line on pattern); for the stocking template, add ½" seam allowance to top edge (dotted line on pattern). Trace outer solid lines to make the lining template.

From red-and-white plaid, cut:
- 1 *each* of Cuff Pattern and Cuff Pattern reversed
- 1—2×7" strip

From solid white, cut:
- 1 *each* of Lining Pattern and Lining Pattern reversed
- 1 of Stocking Pattern reversed

From fusible interfacing, cut:
- 1—18×24" rectangle
- 1 of Stocking Pattern reversed
- 1 *each* of Cuff Pattern and Cuff Pattern reversed

prepare foundation
The Full-Size Embroidery Pattern is on *page 77*.

1 Using a light box or bright window, trace the Stocking Pattern on *Pattern Sheet 2*, including the elf shoes, onto the antique white linen 18×24" rectangle with an air- or water-soluble fabric pen.

2 Place the traced linen rectangle atop the desired boy or girl image of the Full-Size Embroidery Pattern, aligning traced shoes with shoes on embroidery pattern. Trace all design lines to make an embroidery foundation.

embroider foundation

Refer to Basic Stitches, beginning on *page 154,* for stem stitch and straight stitch instructions.

1. Layer embroidery foundation atop interfacing 18×24" rectangle; fuse together following manufacturer's instructions.

2. Using three strands of red embroidery floss, stem-stitch along the traced design lines, except for the eyes and mouth. Note: To prevent threads from showing through the fabric, do not carry them across the back of your work between the design areas.

3. Use a single strand of red floss and tiny straight stitches to embroider the eyes and mouth.

4. Cut foundation along the traced stocking lines to make an embroidered unit.

assemble stocking front and back

1. Layer red-and-white plaid cuff piece atop interfacing cuff piece; fuse together to make front cuff unit. Using cuff reversed pieces, repeat to make the back cuff unit.

2. Sew front cuff unit to the top edge of embroidered unit to make the stocking front. Press seam toward front cuff unit.

3. Layer solid white stocking reversed piece atop interfacing stocking reversed piece; fuse together. Sew the back cuff unit to the top edge of the fused layers to make the stocking back. Press seam toward back cuff unit.

finish stocking

1. Fold red-and-white plaid 2×7" strip in half lengthwise with right side inside. Using ¼" seam allowance, join the long raw edges. Turn right side out and press. Fold the strip in half crosswise, matching the raw edges, to make a hanging loop.

2. Layer solid white lining piece atop stocking front; place hanging loop between the layers (on heel side of cuff), matching raw edges. Sew along top cuff edge to make lined front unit. Press seam open. Repeat with solid white lining reversed piece and stocking back (excluding the hanging loop) to make the lined back unit.

3. Open the lined front and back units. Layer the opened units with right sides together; lining pieces should be together. Sew around the outer edges, leaving a 4" opening in the lining for turning.

4. Turn pieces right side out through opening and press. Slip-stitch opening closed. Push lining to the inside and press the top edge to complete the stocking.

Elfin Stockings
Full-Size Embroidery Pattern

sparkle and shine

Pretty in shades of cream, you'll want to stitch a tree full of these felted wool star ornaments. DESIGNER **ROBIN NELSON**

materials
for one large and one small ornament

- 10" square cream felted wool (stars, hearts)
- Lightweight fusible web
- Metallic embroidery floss: silver
- Rayon embroidery floss: shiny cream
- Embroidery needle
- 2—8-millimeter pearl beads
- 33—4-millimeter pearl beads
- 10—5-millimeter flat back crystal accents
- 10—3-millimeter flat back crystal accents
- Fabric or crafts glue

Finished ornaments: large, 4½"; small, 3¾"

tip

When selecting fusible web for this project, be sure it is paper-backed and lightweight enough to stitch through. (Some fusible webs are too heavy to sew through.)

cut fabric

Cut pieces in the following order. Patterns are on *page 81*.

To felt your own wool, machine-wash it in a hot-water-wash, cool-rinse cycle. Machine-dry it on high heat and steam-press.

To use fusible web to cut wool shapes, complete the following steps.

1 Lay fusible web, paper side up, over large and small star and heart patterns. Use a pencil to trace each pattern once, leaving ¼" between tracings. Cut out each fusible-web shape roughly ⅛" outside traced lines.

2 Following manufacturer's instructions, press fusible-web shapes onto cream wool; let cool. Cut out wool shapes on drawn lines. Peel off paper backings.

From remaining cream wool, cut:
- 1 *each* of large star and small star patterns (without fusible web)

embellish stars

Refer to Basic Stitches, beginning on *page 154*, for featherstitch and blanket stitch instructions. Use three strands of embroidery floss for all stitches.

1. Referring to **Diagram 1**, use silver floss to featherstitch the cream wool large star without fusible web from each tip to the center.

DIAGRAM 1

2. Following manufacturer's instructions, fuse cream wool large heart in center of star (**Diagram 2**). Using shiny cream floss, blanket-stitch around the heart.

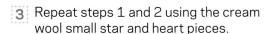

DIAGRAM 2

3. Repeat steps 1 and 2 using the cream wool small star and heart pieces.

4. Referring to photo, *above,* and using fabric or crafts glue, attach pearl beads and crystal accents as desired to make embellished stars.

finish ornaments

1. With fusible web inside, lay each embellished star on its corresponding-size fused cream wool star. Place embellished side facedown on a well-padded surface and cover with a pressing paper or cloth; fuse together wool pieces. Use a dry iron and do not move iron when pressing.

2. Using shiny cream floss, blanket-stitch around outer edges of fused stars to complete the ornaments.

Sparkle and Shine
Large Star Pattern

Sparkle and Shine
Small Heart Pattern

Sparkle and Shine
Small Star Pattern

Sparkle and Shine
Large Heart Pattern

swedish noël

Make your home merrier with ribbon embroidery inspired by Swedish yuletide traditions. DESIGNER **LORI HELLANDER**

materials
- Purchased table runner with light-color center
- Air- or water-soluble fabric pen
- 4-millimeter embroidery ribbon: red
- Chenille needle, size 20

embroider table runner

Because the table runner is light in color, special attention should be paid to concealing the stitch transitions on the wrong side of the fabric by weaving the ribbon back through previous stitches.

Refer to "Ribbon Embroidery 101" on *page 26* for straight stitch and French knot instructions. For stitching progression, follow diagrams A–I in the step-by-step photo on *page 85*, which illustrates how the design is worked with the shortest possible transitions between stitches.

1. Tape the Full-Size Embroidery Pattern, *page 84*, to a light box or bright window. Place the table runner atop the pattern and trace the design the number of times desired onto the fabric using an air- or water-soluble fabric pen.

2. To stitch, bring the needle to the front of the fabric at 1 (diagram A, *page 85*) and make a straight stitch. Work a backstitch, bringing the needle up at 2 and taking it through the fabric at the end of stitch 1. Work a backstitch, bringing the needle up at 3 and taking it through the fabric at the intersection of stitches 1 and 2. Work a straight stitch, bringing the needle up at 4 and taking it back down through the fabric at the end of stitch 4.

tip

To keep from pulling a stitch too tightly, place your thumb over the ribbon on the front of the fabric (where it is being pulled to the back) so you can feel the tension on each stitch.

3. Continue embroidering with backstitches and straight stitches, following the numbered sequence and the direction of the arrows in diagrams B–I, and making French knots at dots on the pattern, to make one half of the snowflake.

4. To finish the snowflake, turn the design around 180°. The last stitch on the first half of the snowflake (stitch 26 in diagram I) now becomes stitch 1 on diagram A, and stitch 25 on the first half of the snowflake becomes stitch 2. Stitch the second half of the snowflake, following the numbered sequence on diagrams A–I, beginning with stitch 3.

5. Repeat steps 2–4 to embroider additional snowflakes as desired to complete the table runner.

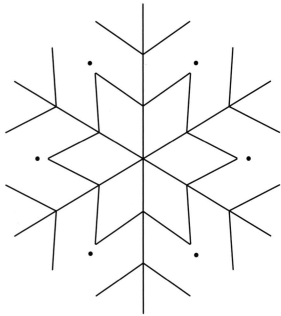

Swedish Noël
Full-Size Embroidery Pattern

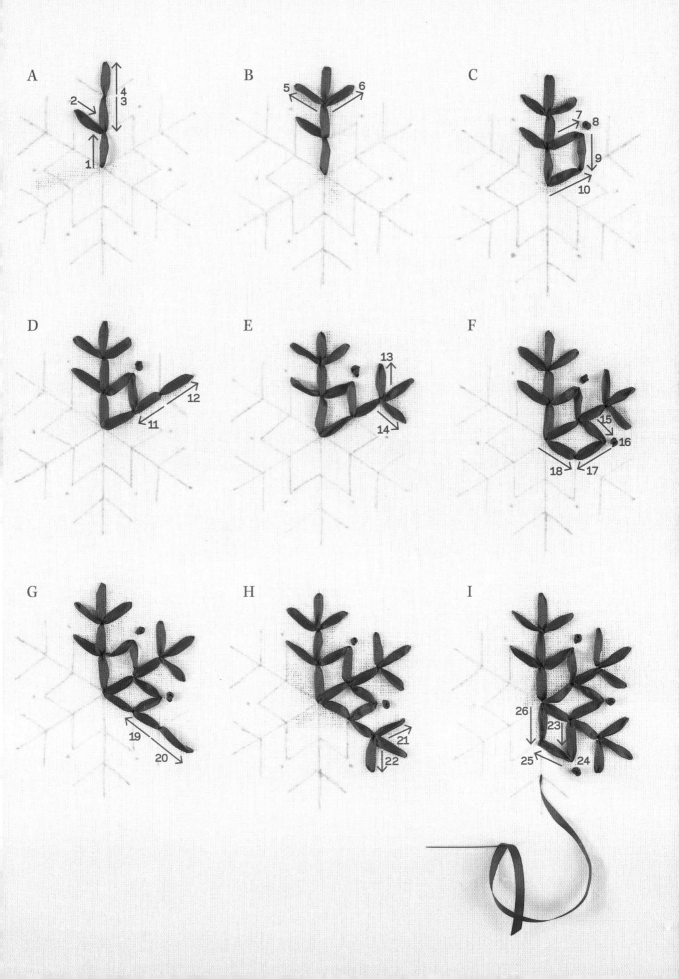

old-world
ornaments

Even if your heritage isn't from the old country, these traditional-inspired ornaments are fun to stitch in fresh colors and felted wool.

DESIGNERS **SARAH HERRMANN** (DALA), **CHERIE WHEELER** (JOY HEART), AND **DANIELLE WILSON** (MATRYOSHKA)

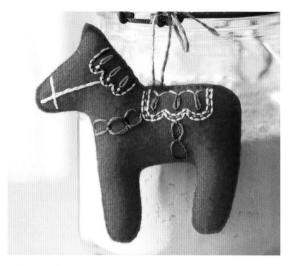

Dala

materials
- 12" square red felted wool (front and back units)
- Tracing paper
- Transfer paper
- Embroidery floss: white, blue, yellow, red
- Embroidery needle
- Polyester fiberfill
- ⅓ yard twine

Finished ornament: 3½" square

cut fabric
To felt your own wool, machine-wash it in a hot-water-wash, cool-rinse cycle. Machine-dry it on high heat and steam-press.

From red wool, cut:
- 2—6×12" rectangles

embroider front unit
Refer to Basic Stitches, beginning on *page 154*, for backstitch, split stitch, French knot, lazy daisy stitch, running stitch, and straight stitch instructions. Use three strands of embroidery floss for all stitches.

1. Trace the Full-Size Dala Pattern, *page 91,* onto tracing paper. Using transfer paper, transfer pattern outline and all dark design lines onto one red wool 6×12" rectangle.

2. Using white floss, outline the saddle and mane with backstitches, sew bridle with split stitches, and make French knots at dots on mane.

3. Referring to lightweight lines on Full-Size Dala Pattern and using blue floss, make three lazy daisy stitches on saddle, outline the mane with backstitches, and sew threaded running stitches for the belly and chest straps (**Threaded Running Stitch Diagram** on *page 91*).

4. Using yellow floss, make lazy daisy stitches on the mane, running stitches between the white saddle outlines, and straight stitches in a V shape at the top of each saddle lazy daisy stitch.

5. Trim embroidered design ⅛" beyond outer lines to make the front unit.

finish ornament
1. Trace and transfer the Dala Pattern outline, *page 91*, onto the remaining red wool 6×12" rectangle. Trim ⅛" beyond outline to make the back unit.

2. Layer the front and back units with wrong sides together. Beginning at the base of the mane and working counterclockwise, use red floss to join the front and back units with backstitches, stitching ⅛" from edges. When you near the starting point at the base of the mane, stuff the shape with fiberfill and insert ends of twine in opening to make a hanging loop. Continue stitching the opening closed, catching ends of hanging loop in stitches, to complete the ornament.

a bit of history ▶ The Dala is inspired by the carved and painted horses of Sweden. It's considered to be a token of goodwill.

Joy Heart

materials

- 11×14" rectangle 24-count cream linen (embroidery foundation)
- 11×14" rectangle red cotton fabric (backing)
- Embroidery floss: red
- Tapestry needle
- Air- or water-soluble fabric pen
- Polyester fiberfill
- 10"-long piece ¼"-wide sheer ribbon: red

Finished ornament: 6×8"

embroider design

Refer to Basic Stitches, beginning on *page 154*, for cross-stitch and backstitch instructions. Use two strands of red embroidery floss to work stitches over two threads of the fabric.

1. Fold linen 11×14" rectangle in half horizontally and vertically to find the center; press lightly and unfold. Referring to Joy Heart Cross-Stitch Pattern, *Pattern Sheet 2*, use cross-stitches and backstitches to embroider the design on the rectangle.

2. Press the embroidered linen rectangle from the wrong side.

assemble heart unit

1. Referring to the Joy Heart Cross-Stitch Pattern on *Pattern Sheet 2* as a guide, use an air- or water-soluble fabric pen to draw a heart shape on the wrong side of embroidered linen rectangle.

2. Layer the embroidered linen rectangle atop the red cotton 11×14" rectangle with right sides together. Sew on drawn heart line, leaving an opening along one side for turning. Cut out the heart shape ½" beyond stitching line. Clip curves just up to seam line. Turn right side out through opening to make the heart unit.

finish ornament

1. Stuff the heart unit with fiberfill; hand-stitch the opening closed.

2. Fold the 10"-long ribbon in half to make a hanging loop. Hand-sew the ends of the hanging loop to the upper back of the heart unit to complete the ornament.

Matryoshka

materials
- 5×6" piece white felted wool (appliqués)
- Scraps of felted wool in yellow, pink, red, and green (appliqués)
- 8×9" piece turquoise felted wool (front and back units)
- Freezer paper
- Air- or water-soluble fabric pen
- Embroidery floss: black, green, pink, red, yellow, white, turquoise
- Embroidery needle
- Fabric glue
- Polyester fiberfill

Finished ornament: 3×5⅛"

cut fabrics
Cut pieces in the following order. The Full-Size Matryoshka Patterns are *opposite*.

   To felt wool, see Cut Fabric, *page 88.*

   To use freezer paper to cut wool shapes, complete the following steps.

1. Lay freezer paper, shiny side down, over patterns. With a pencil, trace each pattern the number of times indicated in cutting instructions, leaving ¼" between tracings. Cut out freezer-paper shapes roughly ⅛" outside traced lines.

2. Using a hot dry iron, press each freezer-paper shape, shiny side down, onto designated wool; let cool. Cut out wool shapes on drawn lines. Peel off freezer paper.

From white wool, cut:
- 1 *each* of patterns A and D

From yellow wool, cut:
- 1 of Pattern B

From pink wool, cut:
- 2 of Pattern C

From red wool, cut:
- 5 of Pattern E

From green wool, cut:
- 2 of Pattern F

From turquoise wool, cut:
- 2 of Pattern G

embroider front unit
Refer to Basic Stitches, beginning on *page 154,* for backstitch, split stitch, running stitch, French knot, and blanket stitch instructions. Use two strands of embroidery floss for all stitches.

1. Using an air- or water-soluble fabric pen, draw eyes and mouth on white wool A face. Backstitch eyes and mouth using black floss.

2. Use fabric glue to adhere B hair and C cheeks to embroidered A face. Glue E flower petals and F leaves to white wool D apron.

3. Referring to photo, *above left,* use green floss and split stitches to outline F leaves and make leaf veins. Make two rows of green split stitches for the flower stem. Use pink floss to make running stitches just inside the C cheek pieces. Using red floss, make running stitches just inside the E flower petals. Use pink floss to add French knots in the flower center and between the petals.

a bit of history ▶ Russian nesting dolls, called matryoshkas, come in assorted personalities, but perhaps the most beloved is the motherly peasant figure.

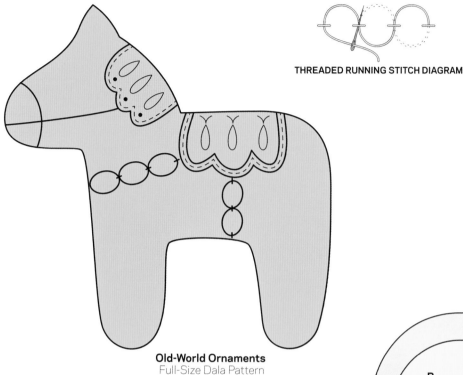

THREADED RUNNING STITCH DIAGRAM

Old-World Ornaments
Full-Size Dala Pattern

4 Glue embroidered A face and D apron to a turquoise wool G body. Referring to photo, use yellow floss to outline the hair with split stitches, and use white floss to add split stitches along lower portion of the face and around the apron. Outline the face and apron again using turquoise floss and split stitches to make the front unit.

finish ornament

1 Cut a 10" length of turquoise floss and fold it in half to make a hanging loop. Glue ends to wrong side of remaining turquoise wool G body at the top of the head to make the back unit. Let glue dry.

2 Layer the front and back units with wrong sides together. Using turquoise floss and blanket stitches, join the units along edges, leaving an opening for stuffing. Stuff with fiberfill and blanket-stitch the opening closed to complete the ornament.

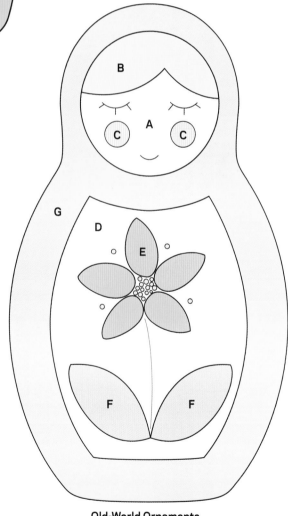

Old-World Ornaments
Full-Size Matryoshka Patterns

holiday HANG-UP

Make nondescript linens worthy of holiday display by embroidering a seasonal design on an inexpensive flour-sack towel. DESIGNER **ELAINE KOONCE**

materials

- Pink flour-sack towel
- Air- or water-soluble fabric pen
- Embroidery floss: white, brown, dark green, light green, burgundy
- Embroidery needle
- Two white four-hole buttons: one ¾" diameter, one 1" diameter

embroider towel

Refer to Basic Stitches, beginning on *page 154,* for running stitch, satin stitch, straight stitch, cross-stitch, and French knot instructions. Use six strands of embroidery floss for all stitches.

1   Using a light box or bright window, trace the Full-Size Embroidery Pattern, *below right,* onto the pink flour-sack towel with an air- or water-soluble fabric pen, centering the design and positioning it 2¼" from the bottom (front) edge of the towel.

2   Use white floss to make running stitches for the snow mounds, and use brown floss to satin-stitch the tree trunk. Make long straight stitches with dark green floss across the width of the tree (the stitches will get shorter as you work from the bottom to the top of the tree). Referring to photo, *right,* add five or six light green straight stitches diagonally over the dark green straight stitches. Note: When stitching the tree, do not carry embroidery threads across the back of your work.

3   Position white buttons as shown on pattern for snowman. Using burgundy floss, make a cross-stitch in the holes of the large "body" button, and make a straight stitch for the mouth in the lower holes of the small "head" button. Using brown floss, make two French knots for the eyes in the upper holes of the small button.

4   Carefully press the finished embroidery from wrong side to complete the towel.

Holiday Hang-Up
Full-Size Embroidery Pattern

holiday *classics*

Stitch up one of these timeless ornaments for your own tree—
or give them as holiday gifts. DESIGNERS **JANICE CORDEIRO** (BAUBLE AND ICE SKATE), **MEGAN BETTS** (TURTLEDOVE)

Needle-Felted Bauble

materials

- Core fiber for felting
- Wool roving: red and white
- Foam pad felting mat
- Felting needles: 38 star needle and 40 triangle needle
- 10"-long piece ¼"-wide satin ribbon: red

Finished ornament: 2¾" diameter

needle-felt ball

1. Lay a core fiber 3×7" rectangle flat on the felting mat and roll it, folding in the sides as you roll and firmly holding it down to express air. Continue rolling it until a ball forms.

2. Using the star felting needle, needle-felt ball until it is firm, rolling it between your hands to keep it rounded. Pull off more core fiber; needle-felt it to the ball until ball measures 2½" in diameter.

3. Using red roving, wrap, needle-felt, and roll ball until it measures 3¼" in diameter. Needle-felt until firm.

wet-felt ball

1. Add two drops liquid dish detergent to 1 cup hot water. Dip the ball into the water. Place the ball in a plastic bag and roll it between your hands for 3 minutes.

2. Turn on hot-water faucet. Remove ball from bag, and as you roll it between your hands, move it in and out of the stream of hot water to remove the soap residue. Machine-dry ball for about 40 minutes. The dry, felted ball will be about 2¾" in diameter.

embroider and finish ornament

1. Pull off a wisp of white roving. Slightly dampen your palms and roll the white roving between them to create a felted string.

2. Cut three 1½"-long pieces of felted string. Using star felting needle, needle-felt strings to ball in a snowflake pattern.

3. Cut six ¾"-long pieces of felted string. Needle-felt pieces to ends of snowflake spokes using the triangle felting needle.

4. For hanger, needle-felt a wisp of red roving to ball over center of red satin ribbon. Knot ribbon ends together to complete the ornament.

Ice Skate
materials
- 11×14" rectangle red felted wool
- 5½" square lightweight cardboard
- Fine-point permanent marker
- Polyester fiberfill
- Perle cotton No. 8: ecru
- Embroidery needle
- 4"-long piece scallop-edge trim: ecru
- Large paper clip

Finished ornament: 2¼×2¾"

cut and assemble skate
To felt wool, machine-wash it in a hot-water-wash, cool-rinse cycle. Machine-dry it on high heat and steam-press.

1. Trace Skate Pattern, *Pattern Sheet 2*, onto cardboard; cut out cardboard template.

2. Fold red wool 11×14" rectangle in half lengthwise to measure 5½×14". Referring to photo, *below*, align bottom of skate template with fold. Use permanent marker to trace along side edges of template. (If desired, you will be able to trace five skates on the folded wool.)

3. Machine-sew on traced lines through both wool layers, leaving top edge unstitched. Cut out skate ⅛" from stitching. Stuff with fiberfill, leaving a small portion at top unstuffed (top is left open).

finish ornament

1. Use ecru perle cotton to make long straight stitches over the center front of the skate for laces, tying a bow at the top. Hand-sew scallop-edge trim around top edge of the skate.

2. Slide paper clip into bottom fold for the blade. Stitch a perle cotton hanging loop to complete the ornament.

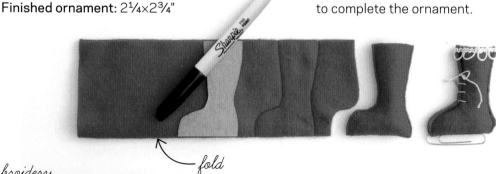

fold

Turtledove
materials
- 9×12" rectangle white felted wool
- Freezer paper
- Embroidery floss: red, white
- Needles: embroidery and chenille
- Polyester fiberfill
- 15"-long piece ⅛"-wide satin ribbon: red

Finished ornament: 4⅜×2½"

cut fabric
Cut pieces in the following order. The Body and Wing patterns are on *Pattern Sheet 2.*

To felt your own wool, see Cut and Assemble Skate, *opposite.*

To use freezer paper to cut wool shapes, complete the following steps.

1. Lay freezer paper, shiny side down, over patterns. Use a pencil to trace each pattern the number of times indicated in cutting instructions, leaving ¼" between tracings. Cut out freezer-paper shapes roughly ⅛" outside traced lines.

2. Using a hot dry iron, press freezer-paper shapes, shiny sides down, onto white wool; let cool. Cut out wool shapes on drawn lines. Peel off freezer paper.

From white wool, cut:
- 1 *each* of Body Pattern and Body Pattern reversed
- 1 *each* of Wing Pattern and Wing Pattern reversed

embroider and finish ornament
Refer to Basic Stitches, beginning on *page 154,* for stem stitch, lazy daisy stitch, French knot, and running stitch instructions. Use one strand of embroidery floss for all stitches.

1. Referring to the Full-Size Turtledove Embroidery Pattern and Stitch Key on *Pattern Sheet 2* for placement, use an embroidery needle and red floss to stem-stitch vines, add lazy daisy stitches for flower petals and leaves, and make French knots for flower centers on each white wool body and wing piece.

2. Using white floss and running stitches, sew embroidered wing and wing reversed pieces to corresponding body pieces to make two bird units.

3. Layer bird units with wrong sides together. Using white floss, join units with running stitches ⅛" from edge, leaving an opening for stuffing. Stuff with fiberfill and stitch opening closed.

4. Thread the red satin ribbon onto the chenille needle. Pull the needle through the bird at X on the pattern. Tie ends in a bow to make a hanging loop and complete the ornament.

tip
If the birds will permanently perch in a wreath, you can embroider just one side. For birds that will hang on a tree, you'll want to stitch each side so they look pretty from any angle.

HO HO HO

Repeat the season's resounding joy and laughter in a sampler
that says Santa is just around the corner. DESIGNER **VICKI HASTINGS**

materials

- 13×19" rectangle 30-count overdyed green linen
- Embroidery floss: white, red, metallic gold, metallic chartreuse, metallic green
- Tapestry needle
- Desired frame

Finished design: 10⅝×5½"

embroider and finish design

Refer to Basic Stitches, beginning on *page 154*, for cross-stitch and backstitch instructions. For white and red stitches, use two strands of the embroidery floss to make cross-stitches over two threads of the fabric. For gold, chartreuse, and green stitches, use one strand of the metallic floss to make the cross-stitches and backstitches over two threads of the fabric.

1. Turn under and baste the edges of green linen 13×19" rectangle to prevent fraying.

2. Fold prepared green linen rectangle in half horizontally and vertically to find center; press lightly and unfold.

3. Referring to Cross-Stitch Pattern and Color Key, *right*, stitch the middle *HO* in the center of the fabric. Then stitch the beginning *HO* and ending *HO*; leave six squares (12 threads) between the repeats.

4. When embroidery is complete, place the design facedown on a soft towel and press using a damp cloth and a warm dry iron.

5. Frame the design as desired.

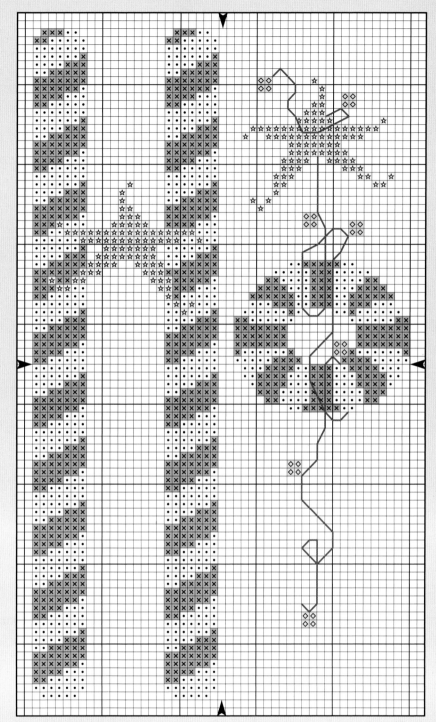

Cross-Stitched Ho Ho Ho
Cross-Stitch Pattern

1 Square = 1 Stitch

COLOR KEY

- ⊡ White
- ⊠ Red
- ✿ Metallic gold
- ◇ Metallic chartreuse
- ╱ Metallic green

GIFTS

Share your love of embroidery by stitching something for someone else. Quick-to-make cards, pretty jewelry, pincushions, bath accessories, and more are great presents for friends and family.

made from
scratch

Satisfy your cravings the no-calorie way with
a dozen yummy doughnut pincushions made from
felt, stitches, and beads.   DESIGNER **LESLEY CHAISSON**

materials
for one pincushion

- 6×12" piece tan, brown, or light brown crafts felt (pincushion body)
- 5" square pink, brown, white, or tan crafts felt (icing appliqué)
- Chopstick (optional)
- Polyester fiberfill
- Sewing thread to match pincushion body
- Perle cotton No. 5 or No. 8: dark pink, cream, white, caramel, yellow
- Embroidery needle
- Assorted bugle or seed beads for embellishing (optional)
- Beading needle

Finished pincushion: Approx. 4" diameter, 1¼" high

Measurements include ¼" seam allowances.

cut fabrics

Cut pieces in the following order.

Patterns are on *pages 106* and *107*. To make paper templates, trace each pattern on paper and cut out. Pin patterns to crafts felt indicated in cutting instructions and cut around the edges.

After cutting out A circle pieces, cut slit and center hole in each as shown on the pattern. Be careful not to cut the center hole too big.

From tan, brown, or light brown felt, cut:
- 2 of Pattern A

From pink, brown, white, or tan felt, cut:
- 1 of Pattern B, C, D, *or* E

assemble pincushion body

1 Layer tan, brown, or light brown felt A pieces with right sides together, aligning edges. Machine-straight-stitch outer curved edges, then inner curved edges, backstitching at beginning and end, to make a tube **(Diagram 1)**.

DIAGRAM 1

2 Turn tube right side out and gently push out edges with a chopstick, if desired, or the eraser end of a pencil.

tip ▶ Make 'em to mimic your favorite pastries by adding appliqué frosting and bead sprinkles.

3 Stuff firmly with fiberfill until tube ends start to come together. Insert one tube end into the other. Using matching sewing thread, slip-stitch overlapped edges together to make pincushion body **(Diagram 2)**. Designer Lesley Chaisson recommends making stitches close together, especially in the center opening, to create a secure seam.

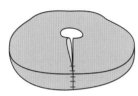

DIAGRAM 2

appliqué and embellish pincushion

Refer to Basic Stitches, beginning on *page 154*, for cross-stitch, whipstitch, blanket stitch, and straight stitch instructions.

1 If desired, stitch large cross-stitches or whipstitches around outer curve of pincushion body using contrasting or matching perle cotton.

2 Position a pink, brown, white, or tan felt B, C, D, or E icing appliqué on pincushion body **(Diagram 3)**.

DIAGRAM 3

3 Using contrasting or matching perle cotton, whipstitch, cross-stitch, or blanket-stitch outer edge of appliqué.

4 Using the same color of perle cotton used in Step 3, whipstitch inner edge of appliqué, pushing appliqué down into curve of pincushion body with your thumb while stitching, to complete the pincushion. Avoid decorative stitches on the inner edge, as this can distort the pincushion.

5 If desired, add "sprinkles" made of perle cotton straight stitches, seed beads sewn on with perle cotton, or bugle beads sewn on with sewing thread. Or, using perle cotton, place vertical straight stitches next to each other to form diagonal lines of "drizzled icing."

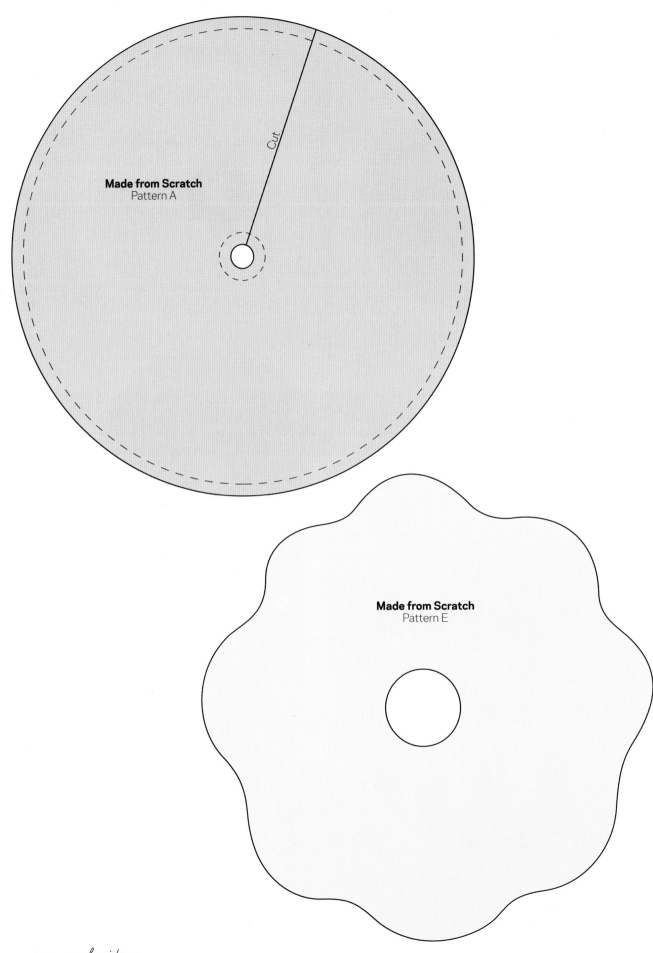

Made from Scratch
Pattern A

Cut

Made from Scratch
Pattern E

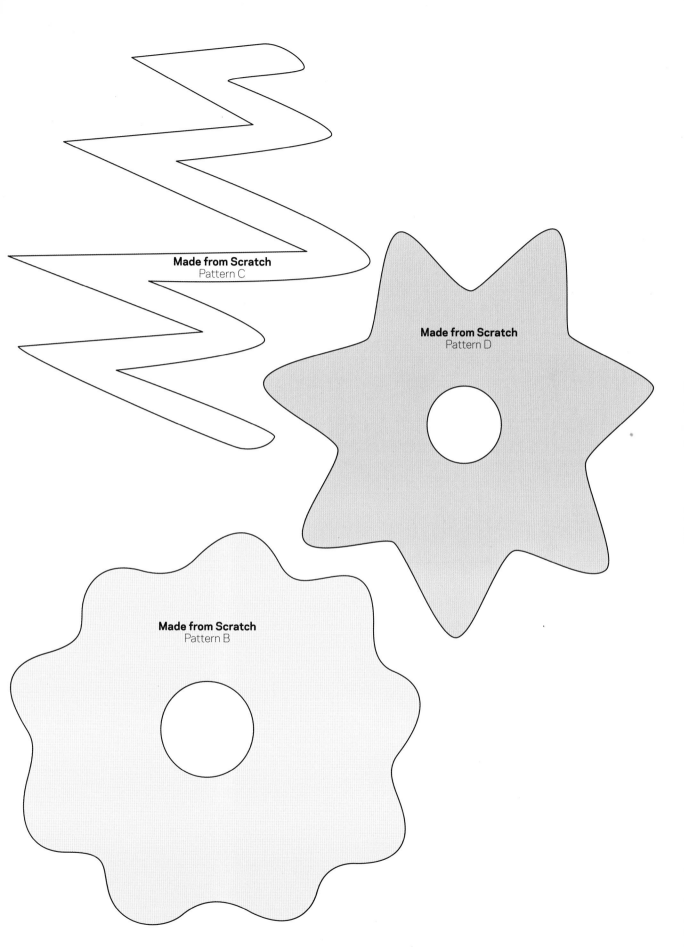

Made from Scratch
Pattern C

Made from Scratch
Pattern D

Made from Scratch
Pattern B

stitched
SENTIMENTS

Why buy mass-produced cards when you can make your own and express your talents at the same time? These whimsical cards use just a few basic stitches in creative ways. DESIGNER **LISA STORMS**

happy birthday to ewe!

thanks a bunch!

get whale soon

"Happy Birthday to Ewe!" Card

materials

- Patterned paper: gold, light blue, light green, pink, yellow
- Solid cardstock: white and black
- Pushpin
- Embroidery floss: white
- Tapestry needle
- Adhesive foam tape

Finished card: 5½×4¼"

assemble card

1 Cut an 8½×5½" rectangle from gold patterned paper. Lightly score the paper in half crosswise; fold along line to make the card base.

2 Cut a 4⅛×2½" rectangle from light blue patterned paper and a 4¾×1" rectangle from light green patterned paper. Trim one long edge of the green rectangle so that it has a wavy edge.

tip

Personalize the card by stitching with floss in the recipient's favorite color; use metallic thread to add a little glitz when you stitch.

3 Using the "Happy Birthday to Ewe!" Card Pattern on *page 113*, cut the sheep body from white cardstock and the face and legs from black cardstock. Cut the hat from pink patterned paper. Use a pushpin to poke random holes into the white cardstock sheep body.

4 Refer to Basic Stitches, beginning on *page 154*, for French knot instructions. Use a tapestry needle and six strands of white embroidery floss to stitch French knots in the sheep body holes.

5 Using the photo, *above*, as a guide, adhere the sheep pieces together and attach them to the light blue patterned paper rectangle using adhesive foam tape. Overlap the green patterned paper rectangle over the sheep legs and attach it with adhesive foam tape.

6 Print "happy birthday to ewe!" onto yellow patterned paper and trim it into a 3¼"-long strip, cutting a notch in each short edge. Attach it to the green patterned paper strip with adhesive foam tape.

7 Attach the light blue patterned paper rectangle to the card base with adhesive foam tape to complete the card.

Change the newsprint paper background and the words on the cardstock strip to convey whatever wishes you want to send.

"Thanks a Bunch!" Card

materials

- Patterned paper: light green and newsprint
- Solid cardstock: white
- Pushpin
- Embroidery floss: dark pink, orange, light pink
- Tapestry needle
- Adhesive foam tape

Finished card: 4¼" square

assemble card

1. Cut an 8½×4¼" rectangle from light green patterned paper. Lightly score the paper in half crosswise; fold along line to make the card base.

2. Cut a 3⅝" square from newsprint patterned paper. Using the "Thanks a Bunch!" Card Embroidery Pattern on *page 113*, transfer the flower center dots and the dots on petals onto the newsprint square. Poke holes through dots with a pushpin.

3. Refer to Basic Stitches, beginning on *page 154*, for lazy daisy stitch and French knot instructions. Wrap floss around needle two times for a double-wrapped French knot. Use a tapestry needle and six strands of embroidery floss for all stitches.

   Make lazy daisy stitches for petals; stitch the large flower with dark pink floss, the medium flower with orange floss, and the small flower with light pink floss.

   Make double-wrapped French knots for the flower centers, using light pink floss for the large flower center, dark pink floss for the medium flower center, and orange floss for the small flower center.

4. Attach the embroidered newsprint square to the card base using adhesive foam tape.

5. Print "thanks a bunch!" onto white cardstock and trim it into a 2¼"-long strip. Cut a notch in the left-hand short edge. Attach the strip to newsprint square using adhesive foam tape to complete the card.

"Get Whale Soon" Card

materials

- Patterned cardstock: green
- Solid cardstock: light blue, aqua, orange
- Crafts glue
- Whale die cut or sticker
- Pushpin
- Embroidery floss: light blue
- Tapestry needle
- Adhesive foam tape

Finished card: 4¼×5½"

assemble card

1. Cut an 8½×5½" rectangle from green patterned cardstock. Lightly score the cardstock in half crosswise; fold along line to make the card base.

2. Cut a 3¼×4½" rectangle from light blue cardstock and a 3⅜×1½" rectangle from aqua cardstock. Using crafts glue, adhere the aqua piece to the bottom of the light blue piece to make the front unit.

3. Temporarily place the whale shape on the front unit. Using the "Get Whale Soon" Card Embroidery Pattern on *page 113,* transfer dots onto front unit so that they are positioned above the whale. Remove whale shape. Poke holes through dots with a pushpin.

4. Refer to Basic Stitches, beginning on *page 154,* for backstitch and French knot instructions. Wrap floss around needle two times for a double-wrapped French knot. Use a tapestry needle and six strands of light blue embroidery floss for all stitches.

Backstitch the spout lines by stitching through the holes. Stitch three double-wrapped French knots to make water drops.

5. Using adhesive foam tape, adhere the embroidered front unit onto the folded card base, and adhere the whale shape below the stitched water spout.

6. Print "get whale soon" onto orange cardstock and trim it into a 2½"-long strip. Cut a notch in the left-hand short edge and adhere it to the front unit with adhesive foam tape to complete the card.

tip

For a light-hearted expression to recognize an achievement, edit the message shown *above* to read "Whale Done!"

"Hi" Card

materials

- Patterned paper: light pink, light blue, yellow
- Solid cardstock: dark pink and coral
- Pushpin
- Embroidery floss: variegated coral and white
- Tapestry needle
- Butterfly punches: small and large
- Adhesive foam tape

Finished card: 5½×4¼"

tip

Sew and store! The stitching on this greeting card is simple enough that you can produce several ahead of time and have them ready to send whenever the need arises.

assemble card

1 Cut an 8½×5½" rectangle from light pink patterned paper. Lightly score the paper in half crosswise; fold along line to make the card base.

2 Cut a 4⅞×3⅝" rectangle from light blue patterned paper. Using the "Hi" Card Embroidery Pattern, *opposite*, transfer dots onto the light blue rectangle. Poke holes through dots using a pushpin.

3 Refer to Basic Stitches, beginning on *page 154*, for backstitch and running stitch instructions. Backstitch the word "hi" through the holes using six strands of variegated coral embroidery floss. Embroider the butterfly's flight path through the holes using six strands of white floss and running stitches.

4 Punch a small butterfly shape from dark pink and coral cardstock and a large butterfly from yellow patterned paper. Adhere butterfly shapes to the stitched rectangle with adhesive foam tape.

5 Attach the stitched rectangle to the card base using adhesive foam tape to complete the card.

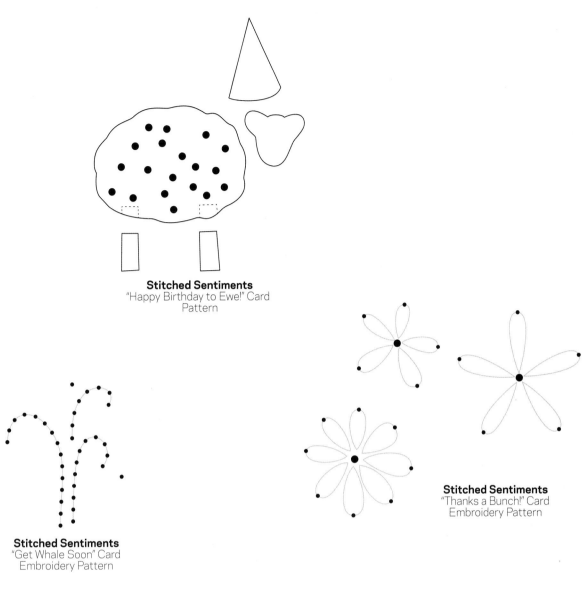

Stitched Sentiments
"Happy Birthday to Ewe!" Card
Pattern

Stitched Sentiments
"Get Whale Soon" Card
Embroidery Pattern

Stitched Sentiments
"Thanks a Bunch!" Card
Embroidery Pattern

Stitched Sentiments
"Hi" Card
Embroidery Pattern

wrap IT UP

Scarves have graduated from wintertime accessories to anytime must-haves. The subtle fabric stripes on one side act as a guide to add large running-stitch accents along the length of the scarf. DESIGNER **JENNIFER KELTNER**

cut fabrics

From *each* red stripe and woven cotton linen, cut:

- 2—13×32" rectangles (with stripes running lengthwise on red stripe)

embroider and finish scarf

1. Machine-sew together red stripe rectangles along the short edges to make a 13×63½" strip. Press seam open. Repeat with the woven cotton linen rectangles.

2. Layer the red stripe strip and woven cotton linen strip. Machine-sew together along long edges, leaving short edges unstitched. Turn right side out; press. If desired, pin along some of the red stripes to secure the layers while hand sewing.

3. Refer to Basic Stitches, beginning on *page 154*, for running stitch instructions. Using embroidery needle, thread approximately 18" of variegated red perle cotton and tie a knot.

4. Starting about ½" from a short edge on the red stripe side, hand-sew long running stitches along a stripe. When you run out of thread, finish with a knot on the red stripe side and begin again with another length of perle cotton. Repeat to sew along as many stripes as desired.

5. Topstitch ¼" from raw short edges, using red thread in the machine needle and cream thread in the bobbin. Pull out a few threads along each raw edge to create a frayed finish, *above left,* and complete the scarf.

materials

- 1 yard red stripe*
- ¾ yard woven cotton linen
- Perle cotton No. 8: variegated reds
- Embroidery needle

*Note: Because the stripe on our fabric runs parallel to the selvage, extra yardage was required to allow for only one seam. If you are not using a directional or stripe fabric, you need only ¾ yard.

Finished scarf: 63½×12½"

Yardages and cutting instructions are based on 42" of usable cotton fabric width and 54" of usable linen fabric width. **Measurements** include ¼" seam allowances. Sew with right sides together unless otherwise stated.

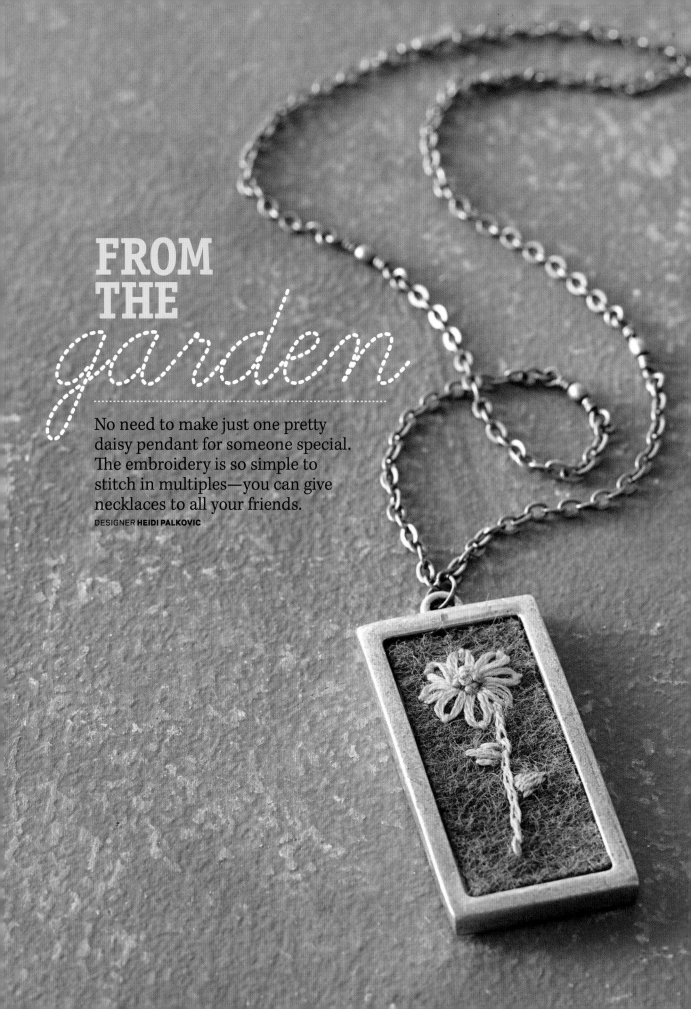

FROM THE *garden*

No need to make just one pretty daisy pendant for someone special. The embroidery is so simple to stitch in multiples—you can give necklaces to all your friends.

DESIGNER **HEIDI PALKOVIC**

materials

- Scrap of gray felted wool
- Chalk pencil
- Embroidery floss: green, yellow, gold
- Embroidery needle
- Small paintbrush
- Crafts glue
- Rectangular necklace pendant (pendant shown has a ¾×1¾" opening)
- Jump ring
- Necklace chain
- Necklace clasp

Finished pendant: ¾×1¾"

embroider and finish pendant

To felt your own wool, machine-wash it in a hot-water-wash, cool-rinse cycle. Machine-dry it on high heat and steam-press.

Refer to Basic Stitches, beginning on *page 154,* for running stitch, chain stitch, satin stitch, lazy daisy stitch, and French knot instructions. Wrap floss around needle two times for a double-wrapped French knot. Use three strands of embroidery floss for all stitches.

1 Measure the opening of the necklace pendant. Using sewing thread, hand-stitch long running stitches onto gray wool to mark the same dimensions. Note: The running stitches will be used as a guide for centering your embroidery and will be removed later.

2 Referring to Full-Size Embroidery Pattern, *right,* lightly mark the flower stem and flower onto gray wool with a chalk pencil, positioning it as desired inside the running stitch design area.

3 Chain-stitch the flower stem using green floss. Satin-stitch the leaves with green floss. Using yellow floss, add lazy daisy stitches at the top of the stem to make an eight-petal flower, leaving a small area unstitched for the flower center. Use gold floss to add four or five double-wrapped French knots in the flower center.

4 When all embroidery is complete, trim the wool to the pendant dimensions, cutting through the running stitch lines.

5 Use a small paintbrush to brush a very thin layer of crafts glue along the inner edge of the necklace pendant. Lightly press the trimmed embroidery design inside the pendant.

6 Attach a jump ring to the pendant loop. Cut the necklace chain into two pieces of desired length. Attach one end of each chain piece to the jump ring, then attach the necklace clasp to the other chain ends to complete the pendant.

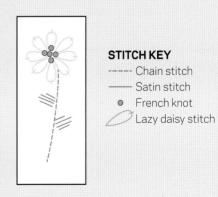

From the Garden
Full-Size Embroidery Pattern

STITCH KEY
------- Chain stitch
——— Satin stitch
● French knot
⬭ Lazy daisy stitch

stuffed mushroom

This little mushroom-shape needle case has two pages for pins and needles and a pocket for scissors, floss, thread, or a thimble. Embellishing it is easy with just one stitch—the blanket stitch.

DESIGNER **MONICA SOLORIO-SNOW**

materials

- 4×12" rectangle red felted wool (mushroom cap)
- 5×20" rectangle white felted wool (stem pocket, appliqués)
- ½×3" strip aqua felted wool (loop)
- Freezer paper
- Embroidery floss: red and white
- Embroidery needle

Finished needle case: 5×6½" (excluding loop)

cut fabrics

Cut pieces in the following order. Patterns are on *page 121*.

To felt your own wool, machine-wash it in a hot-water-wash, cool-rinse cycle. Machine-dry it on high heat and steam-press.

To use freezer paper to cut wool shapes, complete the following steps.

1 Lay freezer paper, shiny side down, over patterns. Use a pencil to trace each pattern the number of times indicated in cutting instructions, leaving ¼" between tracings. Cut out freezer-paper shapes roughly ⅛" outside traced lines.

2 Using a hot dry iron, press each freezer-paper shape, shiny side down, onto designated wool; let cool. Cut out wool shapes on drawn lines. Peel off freezer paper.

From red wool, cut:
- 2 of Pattern D

From white wool, cut:
- 1 *each* of patterns A and B
- 2 of Pattern C
- 9 of Pattern E

embroider and finish needle case

Refer to Basic Stitches, beginning on *page 154*, for blanket stitch instructions. Use two strands of embroidery floss to finish the edges of all wool pieces and assemble the pieces in the following steps.

1 Using red floss, blanket-stitch a red wool D mushroom cap to white wool A stem beginning at green dot and ending at white dot (Diagram 1).

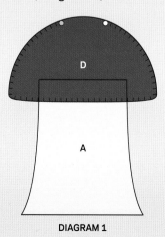

DIAGRAM 1

2   Using white floss, blanket-stitch top edge of white wool B stem beginning at green dot and ending at white dot (Diagram 2).

DIAGRAM 2

3   Using white floss, blanket-stitch white wool B stem to white wool A stem beginning at green dot and ending at white dot, joining side and bottom edges of stem pieces, to make stem pocket and mushroom back (Diagram 3).

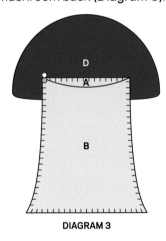

DIAGRAM 3

tip

When appliquéing with wool, use tiny dots of fabric-basting glue to secure small pieces in place before stitching.

4   Using white floss, blanket-stitch around the outer edges of each white wool C piece.

5   Referring to **Appliqué Placement Diagram**, position white wool E circles on remaining red wool D mushroom cap. Trim circles at edges even with mushroom cap. Using white floss, blanket-stitch around white wool E circles.

APPLIQUÉ PLACEMENT DIAGRAM

6   Fold aqua wool ½×3" strip in half to make a loop. Place mushroom back, pocket side up, on flat surface. Referring to **Diagram 4**, stack white wool C pieces together and position on mushroom back. Insert aqua wool loop between C pieces with ends extending into center of C pieces approximately ¼". Position appliquéd D piece on top; pin layers together.

DIAGRAM 4

7   Using red floss, blanket-stitch edge of appliquéd D piece beginning at green dot and working counterclockwise toward white dot (Diagram 4). At white dot, continue blanket-stitching through all layers to join pieces. End stitching at green dot to complete the needle case.

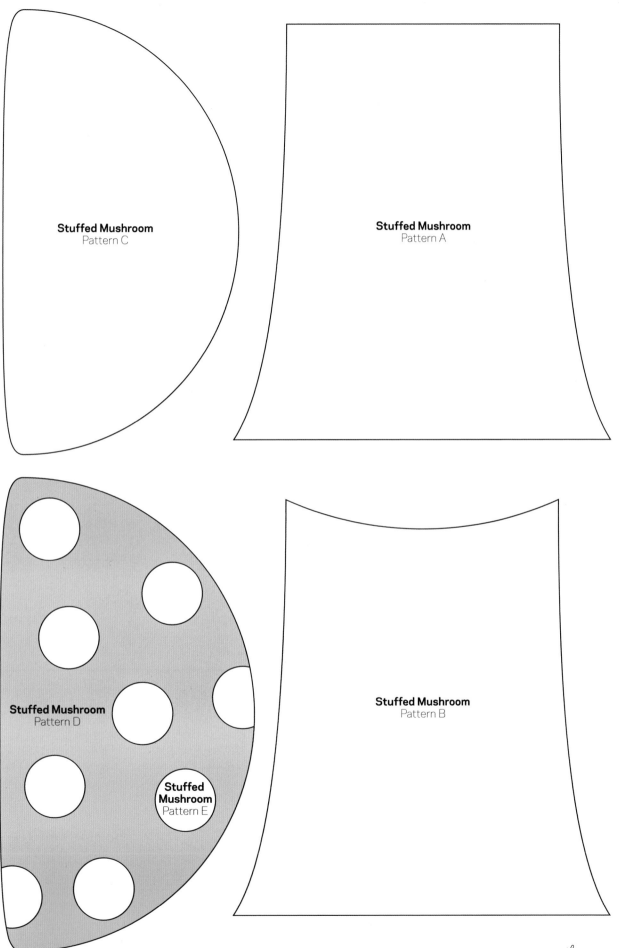

Stuffed Mushroom
Pattern C

Stuffed Mushroom
Pattern A

Stuffed Mushroom
Pattern D

Stuffed Mushroom
Pattern E

Stuffed Mushroom
Pattern B

vintage *style*

Make this scalloped-edge brooch with stacks of pretty felt and sweet stitching to show off a favorite vintage button. DESIGNER **MELISSA DAVISON**

materials

- 5×10" piece green crafts felt (brooch body)
- 5" square *each* of white, pink, and blue crafts felt (appliqués)
- Embroidery floss: red, blue, light pink
- Embroidery needle
- 2—⅜"-diameter buttons: blue
- Vintage ⅞"-diameter button: pink
- Pin back

Finished brooch: 3¾×3"

cut fabrics

Cut pieces in the following order.

Patterns are on *Pattern Sheet 2*. To make paper templates, trace each pattern on paper and cut out. Pin patterns to crafts felt indicated in cutting instructions and cut around the edges.

From green felt, cut:
- 2 of Pattern A

From white felt, cut:
- 1 *each* of patterns B and H

From pink felt, cut:
- 1 of Pattern C
- 2 *each* of patterns D, E, and F

From blue felt, cut:
- 1 of Pattern G

assemble and embellish brooch

Refer to Basic Stitches, beginning on *page 154*, for backstitch, lazy daisy stitch, straight stitch, and French knot instructions. Wrap floss around needle one time for a single-wrapped French knot. Use two strands of embroidery floss for all stitches. When adding embroidery stitches, stitch through all layers to join the pieces.

1 Referring to **Appliqué Placement Diagram**, position B–H appliqué pieces atop one green felt A piece, layering them as shown. When you are happy with the arrangement, temporarily remove both F pieces and the G and H pieces.

2 Use red floss and lazy daisy stitches to embellish bottom edge of the white felt B piece. Use blue floss to backstitch along curved edges of pink felt C, D, and E pieces.

3 Replace both pink felt F pieces and use red floss to backstitch along edges of each piece. Add a single-wrapped red French knot at each scallop indentation.

4 Replace G and H pieces; pin in place. Use red floss to backstitch along edges of the white felt H piece. Add a single-wrapped red French knot at each scallop indentation.

5 Use light pink floss to add straight stitches, lazy daisy stitches, and single-wrapped French knots to the blue felt G piece.

6 Referring to photo, *opposite*, stitch a blue button to the center of each pink felt F piece using blue floss. Sew a vintage button to the center of the H piece to make the brooch body. Note: If you are using a button with holes rather than a shank, use matching floss to stitch it to the felt.

7 Hand-sew the pin back to wrong side of remaining green felt A piece. Layer the brooch body and A piece with the pin back facing out; align edges and pin pieces together. Using blue floss, backstitch just inside the edges through both layers to complete the brooch.

STITCH KEY
- - - - - Backstitch
——— Straight stitch
● French knot
⬭ Lazy daisy stitch

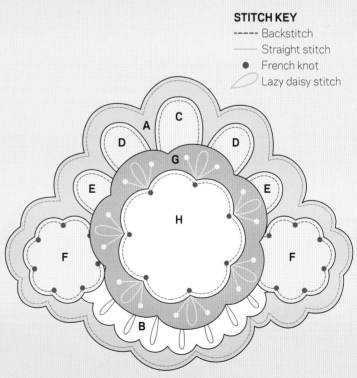

APPLIQUÉ PLACEMENT DIAGRAM

on the *border*

Update the look of cross-stitch with big, airy stitches on a plain linen towel. Rather than follow a chart, trace the Xs directly onto the towel and use six strands of floss for the embroidery. DESIGNER **SHERRI K. FALLS**

materials
- Linen hand towel: ivory
- Air- or water-soluble fabric pen
- 1"-wide gingham ribbon: orange
- Embroidery floss: orange
- Embroidery needle

embroider towel

1. Using a fabric pen and a ruler, mark a line 1½" from the bottom edge of the towel.

2. Trim the ribbon so it is 1½" longer than the width of the towel. Center and pin ribbon along the line, turning ribbon ends under so the folded edges are flush with the side edges of the towel.

3. Topstitch along top and bottom edges of the ribbon.

4. Fold the towel in half lengthwise and finger-press to mark the center. Using the Cross-Stitch Pattern on *Pattern Sheet 3*, trace the design onto the towel with a fabric pen, positioning the tallest column of Xs along the center crease and aligning the bottom row of Xs along top edge of the ribbon.

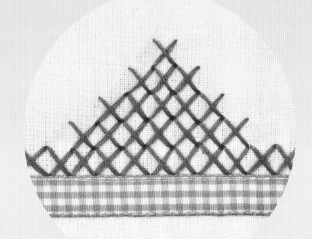

5. Refer to Basic Stitches, beginning on *page 154*, for cross-stitch instructions. Using six strands of orange embroidery floss, cross-stitch the design to complete the towel.

feather your nest

Celebrate summer with a nest full of delightful pincushions.
Vintage wooden spools make these feathered fancies stand tall.
Stitch a flock in a variety of bright-color wools to add light,
practical accents to any sewing area.   DESIGNER **KIMBER MITCHELL VAN HEUKELOM**

materials
for pink pincushion

- 2—4½×7" pieces pink felted wool (bird body)
- 6" square green felted wool (wings, trim)
- Freezer paper
- Chopstick (optional)
- Polyester fiberfill
- 1¼×1¾" vintage wooden thread spool
- Fabric glue
- Perle cotton No. 8: pink
- Embroidery needle
- Rotary cutter with zigzag blade *or* pinking shears
- Long, sharp needle (such as a dollmaker's needle)
- Sewing thread: pink and black
- 2—⅜"-diameter buttons: pink
- 2—4-millimeter round beads: black

Finished pincushion: 5½×5¼×1¾"

Measurements include ¼" seam allowances. Sew with right sides together unless otherwise stated.

cut fabrics
Cut pieces in the following order.

Patterns are on *page 129.* Do not add ¼" seam allowance to Pattern B.

To felt your own wool, machine-wash it in a hot-water wash, cool-rinse cycle. Machine-dry it on high heat and steam-press.

To use freezer paper to cut wool shapes, complete the following steps.

1 Lay freezer paper, shiny side down, over patterns. Use a pencil to trace each pattern the number of times indicated in cutting instructions, leaving ¼" between tracings. Cut out freezer-paper shapes roughly ⅛" outside traced lines.

2 Using a hot dry iron, press each freezer-paper shape, shiny side down, onto designated wool; let cool. Cut out wool shapes on drawn lines. Peel off freezer paper.

From pink wool, cut:
- 2 of Pattern A

From green wool, cut:
- 2 of Pattern B
- 1—1×6" strip

assemble pincushion

1 Sew together pink wool A pieces, leaving a 1½" opening for turning **(Diagram 1).** Backstitch at beginning and end of the seam. Clip the curves. Turn right side out. If desired, use a chopstick to push out the curved corners, such as the tail and beak.

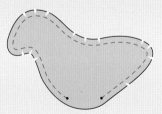

DIAGRAM 1

2 Stuff firmly with fiberfill to make the bird body, leaving about ¼"–½" of space to insert the spool top into the opening.

If you prefer, you can make French knots with black embroidery floss for the eyes instead of using small black beads. See *page 156* for French knot instructions.

3 Test fit of spool by inserting it into base of bird body; it should be snug enough that the spool will not come out once inserted **(Diagram 2)**. If it is too tight, loosen a few threads; if it is too loose, add a few stitches.

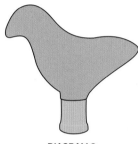

DIAGRAM 2

4 Apply a small amount of fabric glue to one end of the spool. Insert the spool into the opening to make pincushion.

finish pincushion

Refer to Basic Stitches, beginning on *page 154,* for running stitch and blanket stitch instructions.

1 Turn under a scant ¼" seam allowance at the base of the bird body using a needle **(Diagram 3)**. Using pink perle cotton and running stitches, gather seam allowance about ⅛" from edge. Double-knot perle cotton at the end to secure the stitching.

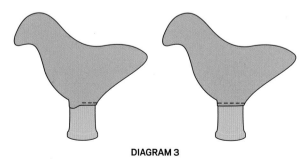

DIAGRAM 3

2 Using a rotary cutter with zigzag blade or pinking shears, trim one long edge of green wool 1×6" strip **(Diagram 4)**.

DIAGRAM 4

3 Referring to photo on *page 126,* wrap green wool strip around gathered bird body base, covering the gathering stitches. Trim excess so the ends meet.

4 Remove green wool strip and apply fabric glue to wrong side along straight edge of strip. Rewrap strip around bird body base, starting at back seam **(Diagram 5)**. Press firmly to adhere strip to base. (If desired, you can glue a narrow accent strip on top of strip just added, as shown in photo, *page 127.*)

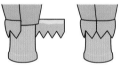

DIAGRAM 5

5 Referring to **Appliqué Placement Diagram,** pin a green wool B wing to one side of the bird body (top of wing will meet seam at top of bird body). Using an embroidery needle and pink perle cotton, blanket-stitch around edge of the wing. Repeat to add remaining wing to the other side of the bird body.

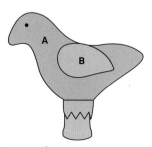

APPLIQUÉ PLACEMENT DIAGRAM

6 Using a long, sharp needle and pink sewing thread, attach a pink button to each wing by passing needle and thread back and forth through the bird body and the holes of each button.

7 Using black sewing thread, repeat Step 6 to attach black beads to the head for the eyes to complete the pincushion.

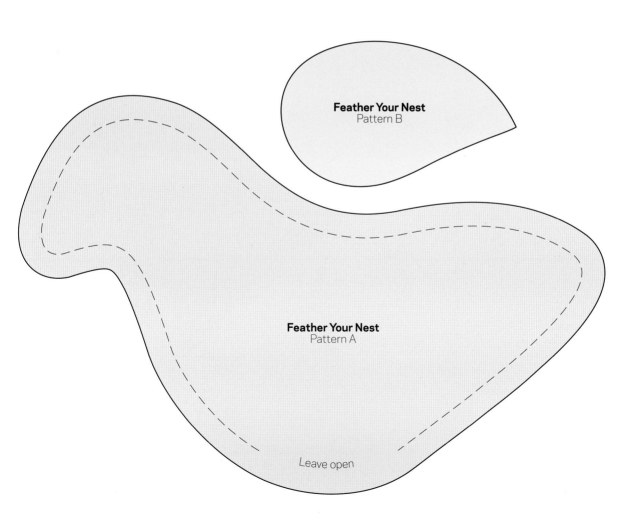

Feather Your Nest
Pattern B

Feather Your Nest
Pattern A

Leave open

*asian*influence

Take inspiration from traditional Japanese sashiko embroidery to construct this pieced pillow enhanced with graceful running stitches.
DESIGNER **JENNIFER KELTNER**

materials

- 8—⅛-yard pieces assorted navy blue prints (pillow top)
- ⅜ yard solid navy blue (pillow back)
- Tracing paper
- Transfer paper
- Perle cotton No. 8: white
- Embroidery needle
- Polyester fiberfill

Finished pillow: 14½×12"

Yardages and cutting instructions are based on 42" of usable fabric width. **Measurements** include ¼" seam allowances. Sew with right sides together unless otherwise stated.

cut fabrics

Cut pieces in the following order.

From _each_ of four navy blue prints, cut:
- 1—3¼×6½" strip

From _each_ of two navy blue prints, cut:
- 1—3½×6½" strip

From _each_ of two navy blue prints, cut:
- 1—3½×12½" strip

From solid navy blue, cut:
- 1—15×12½" rectangle

assemble pillow top

1. Join two navy blue print 3¼×6½" strips along short edges to make a 3¼"-wide row. Press seam in one direction. Repeat with remaining navy blue print 3¼×6½" strips to make a second 3¼"-wide row. Using navy blue print 3½×6½" strips, repeat to make one 3½"-wide row.

2. Referring to **Pillow Top Assembly Diagram,** sew together rows and navy blue print 3½×12½" strips to make the pillow top. Press seams in one direction. The pillow top should be 15×12½" including seam allowances.

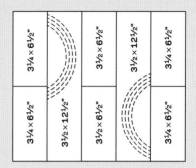

PILLOW TOP ASSEMBLY DIAGRAM

embroider pillow top

1. Using tracing and transfer paper, transfer the Full-Size Embroidery Pattern on _Pattern Sheet 2_ to the pillow top, positioning it on navy blue print 3½×12½" strips as shown in **Pillow Top Assembly Diagram.**

2. Refer to Basic Stitches, beginning on _page 154,_ for running stitch instructions. Using white perle cotton, sew running stitches along marked lines to make an embroidered pillow top.

finish pillow

1. Lay embroidered pillow top facedown on a terry cloth towel and press. (The towel prevents the stitches from getting flattened during pressing.)

2. Sew together embroidered pillow top and solid navy blue 15×12½" rectangle, leaving a 6" opening along one side for turning. Turn right side out to make pillow cover.

3. Stuff pillow cover firmly with fiberfill. Hand-sew the opening closed to complete the pillow.

a bit of history ▶ Sashiko is Japanese folk embroidery that traditionally features white running stitches on a dark blue or black background.

a *head* above

Sweet and simple in lazy daisies and cross-stitches, this felt accessory attaches to an elastic headband. DESIGNER **SANDIE ZIMMERMAN**

materials
- 2—1×12" pieces light gray crafts felt
- Air- or water-soluble fabric pen
- Embroidery floss: beige, terra-cotta, blue-green, gray
- Embroidery needle
- ¼"-wide elastic headband

Finished headband: 1×12" (excluding elastic)

embroider and finish headband

Refer to Basic Stitches, beginning on *page 154*, for lazy daisy stitch, cross-stitch, and running stitch instructions. Use three strands of embroidery floss unless otherwise indicated.

1. Fold a light gray felt 1×12" piece in half crosswise; press lightly to mark center. Referring to the Full-Size Embroidery Pattern, *right*, use a fabric pen to draw the design onto felt piece, aligning A and B dots with center crease.

2. Referring to the pattern, Color Key, and Stitch Key, *right*, use beige and terra-cotta floss to make lazy daisy stitches for the flowers. Use blue-green and gray floss to make cross-stitches.

3. Cut an 11" length from the elastic headband. Pin ends of the 11" headband piece approximately 1" from each short edge of remaining piece of light gray felt. Machine-sew the headband ends in place.

4. Layer the felt pieces with wrong sides together. Trim corners at short ends as shown on the pattern. Using running stitches and one strand of gray floss, sew the pieces together just inside the felt edges to complete the headband.

COLOR KEY
- Beige
- Terra-cotta
- Blue-green
- Gray

STITCH KEY
- 𝒪 Lazy daisy stitch
- ✕ Cross-stitch
- --- Running stitch

A Head Above
Full-Size Embroidery Pattern

*autumn*DUO

Combine felted wool and embroidery to make this leaf and acorn pincushion pair for the sewer on your list. A two-sided acorn tag for holding needles is an added bonus. DESIGNER **ROSEANN MEEHAN KERMES**

Large Pincushion

materials
- 4½×5½" rectangle orange felted wool (leaf appliqué)
- 6×8" rectangle *each* of green plaid and brown felted wools (pincushion unit)
- Scraps of gold and light brown felted wools (acorn tag)
- 2¼×5½" rectangle red felted wool (acorn tag)
- Scraps of assorted wools (circle appliqués)
- Freezer paper
- Embroidery floss: orange, rust, gold, bright green, brown
- Embroidery needle
- Polyester fiberfill

Finished large pincushion: 5⅝×7⅜"

cut fabrics
Cut pieces in the following order. Patterns are on *Pattern Sheet 4*.

To felt your own wool, machine-wash it in a hot-water-wash, cool-rinse cycle. Machine-dry it on high heat and steam-press.

To use freezer paper to cut appliqué shapes, complete the following steps.

1 Lay freezer paper, shiny side down, over patterns. Use a pencil to trace each pattern the number of times indicated in cutting instructions, leaving ¼" between tracings. Cut out freezer-paper shapes roughly ⅛" outside traced lines.

2 Using a hot dry iron, press each freezer-paper shape, shiny side down, onto designated wool; let cool. Cut out wool shapes on drawn lines. Peel off freezer paper.

From orange wool, cut:
- 1 of Pattern A

From green plaid wool, cut:
- 1 of Pattern C

From brown wool, cut:
- 1—5½×7½" rectangle

From gold wool, cut:
- 2 of Pattern D

From light brown wool, cut:
- 2 of Pattern E

From red wool, cut:
- 2 of Pattern F

From assorted wools, cut:
- 14 of Pattern B

1. Referring to **Pincushion Appliqué Placement Diagram**, center orange wool A leaf on green plaid wool C piece; pin in place.

2. Using one strand of orange embroidery floss, whipstitch the edges of the leaf in place, omitting stem.

3. Using one strand of rust floss and a running stitch, double-stitch veins on the leaf.

4. Using two strands of rust floss and a couching stitch, sew stem in place.
   To make a couching stitch, work small stitches, ¼" to ⅜" apart, back and forth over the stem (**Couching Stitch Diagram**).

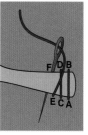

COUCHING STITCH DIAGRAM

5. Referring to **Pincushion Appliqué Placement Diagram**, position assorted wool B circles around edge of green plaid piece; pin in place.

6. Using two strands of gold floss and a star stitch, sew each circle in place.
   To make a star stitch, pull the needle up at A, then push it down at B (**Star Stitch Diagram**). Bring the needle up at C and again push the needle down at B. Pull the needle up at D and again push it down at B. Continue in the same manner around the circle to make a star stitch.

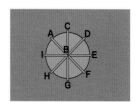

STAR STITCH DIAGRAM

appliqué and assemble pincushion unit

Refer to Basic Stitches, beginning on *page 154*, for whipstitch and running stitch instructions.

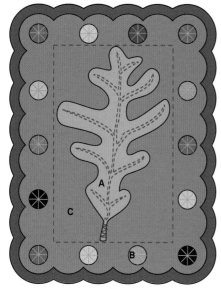

PINCUSHION APPLIQUÉ PLACEMENT DIAGRAM

7 Center and pin appliquéd green plaid piece to brown wool 5½×7½" rectangle.

8 Using two strands of bright green floss and a running stitch, sew through both layers ¾" from scalloped edge, leaving a 1½" opening for stuffing. Do not clip thread.

9 Stuff firmly with fiberfill. Continue stitching both layers together to close opening. Tie off, hiding knot inside.

10 Using one strand of brown floss, whipstitch green plaid scalloped edge to brown wool rectangle. Trim brown wool ¼" away from edge of green plaid piece, following curves of scallops, to make pincushion unit.

appliqué and assemble reversible acorn tag

1 Referring to **Tag Appliqué Placement Diagram**, center gold wool D and light brown wool E pieces on a red wool F oval; pin in place.

TAG APPLIQUÉ PLACEMENT DIAGRAM

2 Using one strand of gold floss, whipstitch edge of D piece to red wool F oval. Using one strand of brown floss, whipstitch edge of E piece in place, omitting stem. Then make Xs where D and E abut to secure top and bottom of acorn together.

3 Using one strand of brown floss, add crosshatch to D piece.

4 Using two strands of brown floss and a couching stitch, sew stem in place to make a tag.

5 Repeat steps 1–4 to make a second tag.

6 Refer to Basic Stitches, beginning on *page 154*, for blanket stitch instructions. Using two strands of bright green floss and a blanket stitch, join tags with wrong sides together to make reversible acorn tag.

finish large pincushion

Referring to photo, *below,* for placement, use six strands of bright green floss to attach reversible acorn tag to pincushion unit, leaving about 1½" of floss between the tag and the stem of the leaf appliqué, to complete the large pincushion.

tip

Felted wool is easy to work with because the edges will not ravel, so there's no need to turn them under.

Small Pincushion

materials

- 10" square dark purple felted wool (background, base)
- Scraps of felted wools in gold check, brown, orange, red, light purple, and bright green check (appliqués)
- Freezer paper
- Embroidery floss: gold, brown, orange, bright green, dark purple
- Embroidery needle
- Polyester fiberfill
- Heavy cardstock

Finished small pincushion: 3½" diameter

cut fabrics

Cut pieces in the following order. Patterns are on *Pattern Sheet 4*.

For details on felting your own wool and to use freezer paper to cut appliqué shapes, see Cut Fabrics, *page 134.*

From dark purple wool, cut:
- 1 *each* of patterns K and L

From gold check wool, cut:
- 1 of Pattern G

From brown wool, cut:
- 1 of Pattern H

From *each* orange, red, and light purple wool, cut:
- 1 of Pattern I

From bright green check wool, cut:
- 1 of Pattern J

From heavy cardstock, cut:
- 1 of Pattern L

appliqué and assemble pincushion top

Refer to Basic Stitches, beginning on *page 154,* for whipstitch and running stitch instructions.

1. Referring to **Acorn Appliqué Placement Diagram** and Appliqué and Assemble Reversible Acorn Tag, steps 1 and 2, *page 137,* whipstitch gold check wool G and brown wool H pieces to dark purple wool K background; use orange floss to make the Xs.

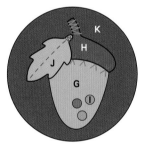

ACORN APPLIQUÉ PLACEMENT DIAGRAM

2. Referring to Appliqué and Assemble Pincushion Unit, Step 4, *page 136,* couch the stem in place using two strands of gold floss.

3. Referring to photo, *above left,* stitch orange, red, and light purple wool I circles to acorn.

4. Referring to **Acorn Appliqué Placement Diagram,** pin bright green check wool J piece in place. Using one strand of bright green floss, sew a running stitch down center of leaf. Using two strands of bright green floss, couch stem in place as before to make the pincushion top.

finish small pincushion

1. Cut sewing thread about 36" long. Thread length through an embroidery needle and knot ends. Work small, even gathering stitches, about ⅛" long, around pincushion top about ¼" from edge. Pull up slightly.

2. With right side down, place a small amount of fiberfill in the center of the pincushion top; position cardstock L circle on top and pull gathers tight around cardstock circle. Secure thread. (Turn pincushion top over to check firmness. You may need to relax gathers and add more fiberfill before securing thread.)

3. Place a small amount of fiberfill in center on the cardstock circle.

4. Position the dark purple wool L base circle over fiberfill (L circle should cover gathering stitches of pincushion top).

5. Using one strand of dark purple floss, whipstitch pincushion top and dark purple wool L circle together along edges to complete the small pincushion.

tip

Use basic hand- or machine-embroidery stitches to attach wool appliqués to an appliqué foundation. For added dimension, tack wool appliqué pieces at their centers only.

relax & revive

Give the gift of relaxation with embroidered at-home spa luxuries.

tip

A purchased bath towel makes a good substitute for the terry-cloth fabric needed for the bath mitt.

Bath Mitt

materials

- ⅓ yard white terry cloth
- 4-millimeter silk embroidery ribbon: blue, dark green, light green, and three shades of lavender
- Chenille needle, size 20
- Satin blanket binding: lavender

Yardages and cutting instructions are based on 42" of usable fabric width. **Measurements** include ¼" seam allowances. Sew with right sides together unless otherwise stated.

embroider mitt front

1. To make the mitt pattern, trace around your hand on paper, beginning and ending near your wrist. Draw again 1½" beyond the traced lines, making a straight line across the bottom of the pattern for the wrist opening. Cut out the mitt pattern along outer lines.

2. Use the mitt pattern to trace and cut one shape (mitt front) and one reversed shape (mitt back) from white terry cloth. Zigzag-stitch or overcast all edges of each terry cloth shape using white sewing thread.

3 Referring to the Bath Mitt Full-Size Embroidery Pattern on *page 145* and "Ribbon Embroidery 101" on *page 26*, embroider the flowers on right side of the mitt front using a chenille needle and silk ribbons.

Make a lazy daisy stitch for each flower petal, stitching one flower from each of two shades of lavender ribbon and one flower from blue ribbon. Use dark green ribbon to ribbon-stitch the stems. Use light green ribbon to add two straight-stitch leaves to each flower and to make a bow of two loop stitches between the stems, adding two small straight stitches in the bow center. Use the third shade of lavender ribbon to add random French knots among the flowers and to make the flower centers.

finish mitt

1 Sew the embroidered mitt front and the mitt back together along curved edges, beginning at the bottom edge on the thumb side and ending 4" from the bottom edge on opposite side.

2 Bind the straight bottom edges with lavender satin blanket binding. Finish the seam on the edge opposite the thumb, leaving the bottom edge open. Turn right side out to complete the mitt.

Renewal Pillow
materials

- ¼ yard *each* of light lavender satin and dark lavender satin
- Air- or water-soluble fabric pen
- Embroidery floss: light lavender
- Embroidery needle
- Polyester fiberfill
- 3 ounces lavender buds

Finished pillow: 9½" long, 3½" diameter

Yardages and cutting instructions are based on 42" of usable fabric width. **Measurements** include ½" seam allowances. Sew with right sides together unless otherwise stated.

cut fabrics

Cut pieces in the following order.

From light lavender satin, cut:
- 1—6½×12" rectangle

From dark lavender satin, cut:
- 2—6½×12" rectangles

embroider rectangle

1 Tape the Renewal Pillow Full-Size Embroidery Pattern on *page 145* to a light box or bright window. Place light lavender satin 6½×12" rectangle atop pattern, centering the pattern lengthwise on rectangle. Use an air- or water-soluble fabric pen to trace the pattern.

2 Refer to Basic Stitches, beginning on *page 154*, for backstitch instructions. Using three strands of light lavender embroidery floss, backstitch along marked lines to make an embroidered rectangle.

finish pillow

1 Sew a dark lavender satin 6½×12" rectangle to each long edge of the embroidered rectangle. Press seams open. Fold the joined rectangles in half lengthwise with right sides together, matching the seam lines. Sew along long edge to make a tube. Press seam open (this seam will be the center back seam). Turn tube right side out.

2 Press under ½" on one open end of tube. Flatten the tube, aligning pressed edges. Using a doubled length of sewing thread, hand-sew long running stitches ¼" from pressed edge. Pull the thread tightly to gather and close the opening; knot thread to secure.

3 Stuff the tube halfway with fiberfill and add the lavender buds. Finish stuffing the tube with fiberfill.

4 Repeat Step 2 with remaining open end of tube to complete the pillow.

Quietude Pillow
materials
- ¼ yard *each* of light blue satin and dark blue satin
- Air- or water-soluble fabric pen
- Embroidery floss: light lavender
- Embroidery needle
- Polyester fiberfill
- 3 ounces lavender buds

Finished pillow: 12×10"

Yardages and cutting instructions are based on 42" of usable fabric width. Measurements include ½" seam allowances. Sew with right sides together unless otherwise stated.

cut fabrics
Cut pieces in the following order.

From light blue satin, cut:
- 5—3×13" strips

From dark blue satin, cut:
- 5—3×13" strips

assemble and embroider strip unit

1. Sew together the light and dark blue satin 3×13" strips along long edges, alternating colors, to make a strip unit; do not sew the first strip to the last strip. Press seams open. The strip unit should be 13×21" including seam allowances.

2. Tape the Quietude Pillow Full-Size Embroidery Pattern, *opposite,* to a light box or bright window. Place strip unit atop pattern, centering the pattern lengthwise on a dark blue satin strip. Use an air- or water-soluble fabric pen to trace the pattern.

3. Refer to Basic Stitches, beginning on *page 154,* for backstitch instructions. Using three strands of light lavender embroidery floss, backstitch along marked lines to make an embroidered unit.

tip

If lavender buds aren't available, substitute dried chamomile, lemon balm, and/or rosemary for soothing and aromatic pillow filling.

finish pillow

1. Sew the last satin strip of embroidered unit to the first strip, creating a tube. Press seam open. Flatten the tube so the embroidered strip is centered on the front side, aligning raw edges and matching seam allowances. Sew together raw edges on each open end of the tube to make pillow cover, leaving a 3" opening on one end for turning.

2. Turn pillow cover right side out through opening. Fill pillow cover with fiberfill and add lavender buds. Hand-sew opening closed to complete the pillow.

Relax & Revive
Bath Mitt
Full-Size Embroidery Pattern

renewal

Relax & Revive
Renewal Pillow
Full-Size Embroidery Pattern

quietude

Relax & Revive
Quietude Pillow
Full-Size Embroidery Pattern

all abloom

Great for perfecting your lazy daisy stitch technique, this lovely felted wool pincushion is brimming with flowers in a variety of sizes and hues.

DESIGNER **SANDIE ZIMMERMAN**

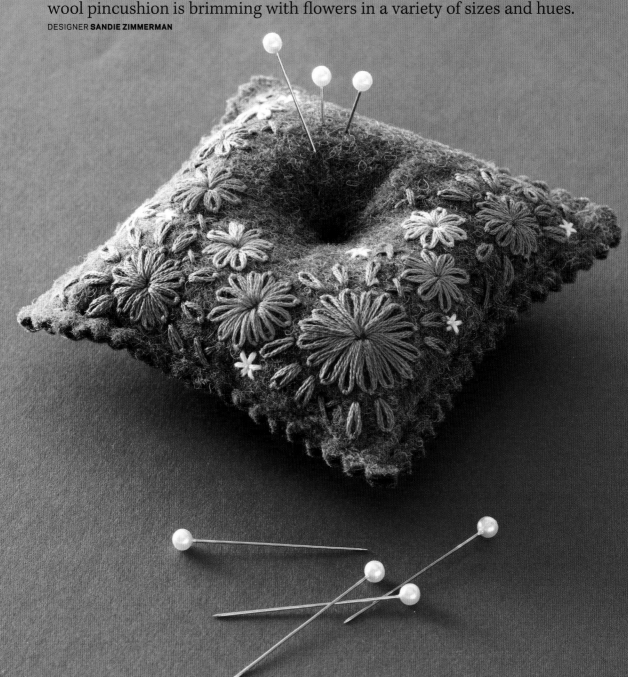

materials

- 4×8" piece blue felted wool
- Pinking shears
- Embroidery floss: blue, cream, light rose, dark rose, gold
- Embroidery needle
- Polyester fiberfill

Finished pincushion: 3½" square

cut fabric

To felt your own wool, machine-wash it in a hot-water-wash, cool-rinse cycle. Machine-dry it on high heat and steam-press.

From blue wool, use pinking shears to cut:
- 2—3½" squares

embroider and finish pincushion

Refer to Basic Stitches, beginning on *page 154*, for cross-stitch, lazy daisy stitch, straight stitch, running stitch, and French knot instructions. Wrap floss around needle two times for a double-wrapped French knot. Use four strands of embroidery floss unless otherwise specified.

1 Referring to Full-Size Embroidery Pattern, *below*, for stitch placement and color usage, make cross-stitches, lazy daisy stitches, and straight stitches on one blue wool 3½" square. Be sure to leave enough space around the square's perimeter for a ⅜" seam.

2 Layer embroidered blue wool square atop remaining blue wool 3½" square with wrong sides together, aligning pinked edges. Using two strands of blue floss, make running stitches to join squares, stitching approximately ⅜" inside the pinked edges. Leave a 2" opening along one side for stuffing.

3 Tightly stuff joined squares with fiberfill through the opening. Sew opening closed with running stitches.

4 Tuft the Step 3 unit by stitching a double-wrapped French knot through the center with blue floss, working from back to front so knot is visible on the back side. Tie off thread and trim ends on back to complete the pincushion.

All Abloom
Full-Size Embroidery Pattern

STITCH KEY
✕ Cross-stitch
⬭ Lazy daisy stitch
✳ Straight stitch
— — Running stitch
• French knot

BASICS

Ready to get started or freshen your embroidery skills?
Discover what tools you'll need, learn how to transfer a pattern,
and find the basic stitches that will ensure your success.

tools

One of the most appealing qualities of embroidery is how little you really need to get started. You might even find that many of the supplies are already in your crafting stash—especially if you are a quilter or a seamstress—but if needed, you can pick up any of the necessary items at a crafts or needlework shop with little investment.

embroidery surfaces

Although you'll find linens, Aida cloth, and other specialty needlework fabrics at crafts stores and needlework shops, you can stitch on virtually anything a needle will pass through. In fact, it's possible to stitch on surfaces other than traditional cotton or linen fabric. Felt, wool, paper, leather, velvet, satin, and decorator fabrics are all fair game. Pre-finished and store-bought items such as tablecloths, runners, and napkins make great stitching candidates, too. And, believe it or not, you can even embroider on wood by stitching through holes you've drilled into the surface.

needles

Think all needles are the same? Before you reach into your sewing basket for your trusted mending needle, think again. While all needles have an eye and a pointed end, not all needles work well for embroidery. The key is to choose a needle that has a large enough eye to accommodate the type of thread you are working with, and to choose a needle that is the proper size for the surface you are stitching on. A needle should be able to make a hole in the fabric that is large enough for the shaft and threaded eye to pass through.

There are three types of embroidery needles: tapestry, chenille, and crewel. Each needle has a long oval eye, which is best for accommodating the thickness of multiple strands of floss, perle cotton, or yarn. Tapestry needles have a blunt end, crewel needles have a sharp end, and chenille needles have a sharp end with a long shank

(chenille needles work well for ribbon embroidery). Each hand-embroidery needle also has a size. The larger the number, the smaller or finer the needle.

So how do you know what needle you need? If you're stitching on a tightly woven fabric, you'll want to choose either a chenille or a crewel needle so that the pointed end can pierce the fabric. If you're working with Aida cloth or an open-weave fabric, the blunt end of a tapestry needle will work best. Many beginner stitchers find that buying a package of assorted sizes—which are often packaged by needle type—is a great way to experiment with different needles to find the right one for the job. Before you start your project, try pushing the needle and thread through the surface to be embroidered several times. If the needle eye catches or is difficult to bring through the surface, the needle size is too large. If your stitches are fine or the area you are working in is tight, you'll find that a shorter needle is a good choice.

threads

Threads are available in more varieties today than ever before. Depending on the look and effect you want to achieve, your options are vast. For beginner purposes, we'll discuss the most popular options: embroidery floss, perle cotton, yarn, and ribbon.

Embroidery floss. Six-stranded embroidery floss is always a popular choice among embroiderers. It's readily available, inexpensive, and comes in hundreds of colors. Sold by the skein, each color from each manufacturer has its own unique number. One of the best parts about embroidery is the freedom to customize any design to your preferred hues and shades. Feel free to pick and choose colors that you like. Just keep in mind that if you run out of a color in the middle of a design, you'll need to remember what number you used so you can match it accurately when you continue stitching.

To use floss, separate the strands (also referred to as "plies" of floss) according to the weight of stitch you'd like to create. Use just one or two plies for fine details, or use all six plies for bold, thick stitches. A suggestion of three or four plies is common for most embroidery designs. You can even combine a few plies from one color with a few plies from another. This is a great way to create a shaded or variegated look.

You'll also find a number of specialty embroidery flosses; overdyed, satin, fluorescent, glow-in-the-dark, and metallic are all options for giving your work highlights, sheen, glitz, and special effects. Just be aware that some specialty threads can be a bit more difficult to work with—but they may be worth the extra effort for the look you wish to achieve.

Perle cotton. This 100% cotton, twisted thread is sold by the skein or by the ball and produces raised, dimensional stitches with a bit of shine. Unlike embroidery floss, it is non-divisible, but it is available in four different weights: size 3, 5, 8, and 12. Size 3 is the thickest and size 12 is the finest. The thickness of your stitches is determined by the weight of the thread used. Size 5 perle cotton is commonly suggested for embroidery. Perle cotton is available in a multitude of colors; however, many crafts stores limit their inventory to more neutral colors. Specialty needlework shops tend to offer more color options in this thread category.

Yarn. Wool is the most popular and sturdy option in this thread category. Crewel projects are stitched with wool yarn on a linen background, producing a warm, textural look.

Ribbon. Ribbon gives basic embroidery stitches an elegant, dimensional look. Narrow silk ribbons are usually the preferable choice for ribbon embroidery and are available in different widths that are indicated in millimeters. A chenille needle works best when stitching with ribbon.

scissors

Not all scissors are the same when it comes to embroidery. A pair of fine-tip embroidery scissors is an essential item for every stitcher's supply basket. Time and again, you'll find those super-sharp points helpful for picking out stitches, trimming thread tails, and cutting off lengths of thread from skeins and balls.

Scissors can vary widely in price and style. If you prefer elegant and traditional, indulge in a pair of lovely gold-handle stork scissors. For the more utilitarian, choose a pair of small scissors from the fabric store without the fancy decorations. Whatever style you choose, just make sure that you keep them sharp and prolong their life by relegating them only to cutting embroidery threads. It's also a good idea to protect your scissors by keeping them inside a scissor holder or a magnetic needle case. Some embroidery scissors come with a leather sheath to protect the super-sharp points.

hoops

Embroidery hoops help keep your fabric taut while you work, making it easier to create uniform stitches.

Hoops come in wood or plastic and have two parts: the inner hoop, which is a continuous ring, and the outer hoop, which has a screw connector for tightening the outer hoop around the inner hoop. If you use a wooden hoop, be mindful of rough edges, which could catch on your fabric and damage your work.

tracing paper

For patterns printed in this book and for other patterns where you want to keep the original pattern intact, it's useful to first make a copy using tracing paper. Lay this transparent paper over the original pattern, then use a pencil or marking pen to trace the design onto the paper.

If you're using light-color fabric for your embroidery, you can lay the fabric right over the tracing paper pattern and trace it again onto the fabric. For darker fabrics and surfaces, use transfer paper to transfer the pattern from the tracing paper to the surface.

transfer paper

Known also as carbon dressmaker's paper, this special paper is useful for transferring patterns onto non-transparent fabrics and surfaces. It works by applying pressure with a stylus or ball-point pen to trace the design onto the paper, resulting in transferred pattern lines on the desired surface.

marking pens and pencils

There are many different types of pens and pencils on the market for marking designs on fabric. Air-soluble fabric pens and water-soluble fabric pens are the most commonly available; however, some find the tip to be a bit cumbersome for transferring detailed designs, and sometimes a chemical residue can cause permanent staining. A soft #2 lead pencil works well, can be laundered out, or can be erased away with a non-marring art eraser.

getting started

transferring a design

Bright window or light box. Once you've selected your design and the surface you wish to embroider, it's time to transfer the design from paper to fabric. If you're working with light-color fabric, all you need is a bright window or a light box.

First lay a piece of tracing paper over the design and trace the design using a pencil or marking pen. Tape the tracing paper to a bright window or a light box, making sure it is flat and secure on all sides.

Next, lay your fabric over the tracing paper, positioning it so the pattern shows through the fabric in the desired location. Using a pencil or fabric pen, trace the design onto the fabric. Use short, light strokes to avoid shifting the fabric while tracing.

Transfer paper. For non-transparent fabrics, such as dark-color woven fabrics, crafts felt, and wool, choose transfer paper to transfer the design to the embroidery surface. This paper also can be used on solid surfaces such as wood.

Before beginning, choose a paper with a color that will be visible against the color of your fabric or surface to be embroidered. Once you've selected your paper, lay it with the colored side down over the surface you wish to embroider, then lay the pattern on top. Use a stylus or a ball-point pen to firmly trace the lines of the pattern, transferring the design to the fabric.

prepare the thread

A good rule of thumb is to cut the thread you wish to stitch to a length equal to your forearm from fingertips to elbow. Too much length will make it hard to keep even stitch tension.

If you're using embroidery floss, it's a good idea to separate the strands before stitching—even if you plan to stitch with all six plies. This process is referred to as "stripping" the floss and will make the floss easier to work with, will help to keep it twist- and tangle-free, and will ensure smoother, more attractive stitches. Simply pinch all of the plies together at the top with one hand, then pull one of the strands out from the top until it is removed from the group. Repeat with each strand until they have all been separated, then put them all back together again and run your fingers down the strands to flatten them out.

hoop the fabric

To put your fabric in a hoop, first lay the inner part of the hoop on a flat surface and center your fabric on top with your design facing up. Loosen the screw on the outer hoop so that it is loose enough to easily place over the fabric. Press the outer hoop down over the inner hoop until the fabric is evenly caught between the two hoops. Adjust the fabric as necessary and tighten the screw until the fabric is taut.

The fabric will naturally loosen as you work, so occasionally you'll need to stop stitching, adjust your work, and retighten the fabric in the hoop. If you plan to be away from your stitching for an extended period of time, remove your fabric from the hoop to prevent excessive stretching and to allow the fabric to relax.

anchor the first stitch

Rather than using a knot, the first embroidery stitches are anchored by other stitches on the back side of your work. Depending on the type of stitch, this can either be done by catching the tail in the back side of the stitches as you work, or by leaving a long tail that can later be threaded through a needle and woven through the back side of nearby stitches.

ending your stitches

When you reach the end of your stitching or are running out of thread, secure the end of your stitches much like you did at the beginning of the process. With the thread still in the needle, weave the needle under a few stitches on the back side of the work, then remove the needle, leaving the remaining thread as a tail. Trim off the excess thread.

basic stitches

With just a few basic stitches, you can create dynamic embroidered effects. Combine the basics and you can elevate the texture and dimension of your designs. Don't be afraid to allow yourself creative leeway—make your own variations and you may be surprised at the results. Follow the step-by-step instructions to learn these 13 essential stitches.

backstitch

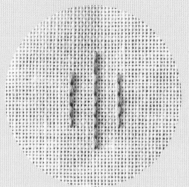

The perfect stitch for outlines, this simple stitch works best when a very precise line is necessary.

To backstitch, pull the needle up at A, insert it back into the fabric at B, and bring it up at C. Continue in the same manner.

BACKSTITCH

blanket stitch

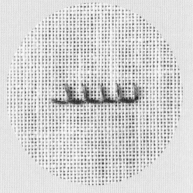

This decorative stitch can be a bit confusing at first, but with a little practice, you'll pick up the overlapping pattern and be stitching it with ease.

To blanket-stitch, pull the needle up at A, form a reverse L shape with the thread, and hold the angle of the L shape in place with your thumb. Push the needle down at B and come up at C to secure the stitch. Repeat for as many blanket stitches as desired. You may wish to make all your stitches the same length, as shown in the illustration, or vary the lengths.

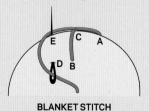

BLANKET STITCH

chain stitch

Versatile as a decorative stitch, outline, or border, this textured stitch is a series of loops joined together to resemble a chain.

To chain-stitch, pull the needle up at A, form a U shape with the thread, and hold the shape in place with your thumb. Push the needle down at B, about 1/16" from A, and come up at C. Repeat for as many chain stitches as desired.

CHAIN STITCH

cross-stitch

Gaining its popularity from charted designs stitched on the uniform squares of Aida cloth, cross-stitch works well for free-form embroidery on other fabrics as well. It's simply two straight stitches, crossed at the centers.

To cross-stitch, pull the needle up at A. Insert it back into the fabric at B, and bring it up at C; then push the needle down again at D.

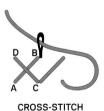

CROSS-STITCH

featherstitch

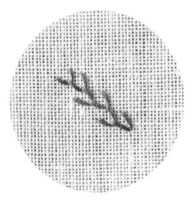

Overlapping V-shape stitches give this stitch its distinctive featherlike look.

To featherstitch, pull the needle up at A, form a V shape with thread, and hold the angle in place with your thumb. Push needle down at B, about 3/8" from A, and come up at C. For the next stitch, insert needle at D and bring it out at E; continue in the same manner.

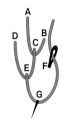

FEATHERSTITCH

french knot

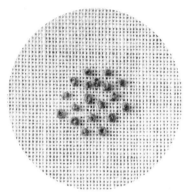

This raised knot makes a nice dimensional accent when stitched alone, sprinkled throughout a design, or grouped together to fill a space.

To make a French knot, bring the needle up at A. Wrap the thread around the needle two or three times without twisting it. Insert the needle into the fabric at B, about 1/16" away from A. Gently push the wraps down the needle to meet the fabric and then pull the needle and thread through the fabric slowly and smoothly.

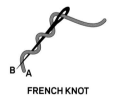

FRENCH KNOT

lazy daisy stitch

One loop, similar to the chain stitch on page 155, is tacked down with a tiny straight stitch to form this versatile stitch. Make one loop for a leaf, or stitch several in a circular pattern to fashion a flower.

To make a lazy daisy stitch, pull the needle up at A and form a loop of thread on the fabric surface. Holding the loop in place, insert the needle back into the fabric at B, about 1/16" away from A. Bring the needle tip out at C and cross it over the trailing thread, keeping the thread as flat as possible. Pull the needle and trailing thread until the loop lies flat against the fabric. Push the needle through to the back at D to secure the loop.

LAZY DAISY STITCH

running stitch

Another simple stitch perfect for borders and outlines, this stitch resembles a dashed line.

To make a running stitch, pull the needle up at A and insert it back into the fabric at B. Continue in the same manner, loading several stitches on the needle at a time.

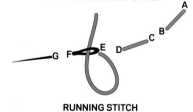

RUNNING STITCH

satin stitch

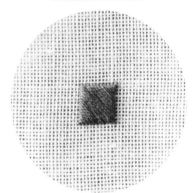

When you want to fill an area with solid stitching, the satin stitch is the perfect choice and is recognized by its closely spaced straight stitches.

To satin-stitch, fill in the design area with straight stitches, stitching from edge to edge and placing the stitches side by side.

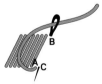

SATIN STITCH

split stitch

Use your embroidery needle to split each previously made straight stitch and create a textured line perfect for flower stems and outlines.

To split-stitch, pull the needle up at A and insert the needle back into the fabric at B, about ⅛"–¼" away from A. Then, holding thread atop the stitching line, bring the needle back up at C, piercing through the center of the first stitch, and pull the thread down at D so it lies flat against the fabric. Continue in the same manner, pulling with equal tautness after each stitch.

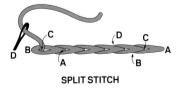

SPLIT STITCH

stem stitch

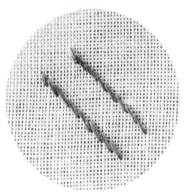

Just as its name implies, this stitch is often used for flower stems and outlines and works well for curved lines.

To stem-stitch, pull the needle up at A. Insert the needle back into the fabric at B, about ⅜" away from A. Then, holding the thread out of the way, bring the needle back up at C, half way between A and B, and pull the thread through so it lies flat against the fabric. Pull with equal tautness after each stitch.

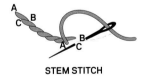

STEM STITCH

straight stitch

whipstitch

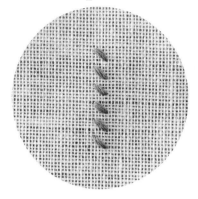

Sometimes all you need is a basic stitch. The straight stitch is just one stitch sewn in any direction.

Another basic stitch, the whipstitch is used to join two finished edges or to attach a shape to a foundation.

To straight-stitch, pull the needle up at A. Insert needle back into the fabric at B. Continue in the same manner.

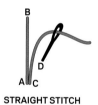

STRAIGHT STITCH

To whipstitch, pull the needle up at A. Insert needle at a diagonal angle through the front edge at B, resulting in a slanted stitch, and picking up only one or two fabric threads at a time. Continue in the same manner.

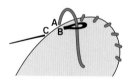

WHIPSTITCH

finishing

Once your embroidery is complete, it's time to turn it over and clean up the back. Use embroidery scissors to trim off dangling thread ends and weave in any long tails if needed.

After you remove your work from the hoop, your fabric will most likely have hoop marks and wrinkles. Most small pieces of embroidery can be pressed with a warm iron. To help preserve the raised texture of the embroidery, lay the embroidered fabric facedown on a white terry-cloth towel and lightly spritz the back with water. With your iron set to a warm setting, gently iron the back of the work.

blocking

Sometimes you'll find that your work has stretched and become distorted while you've been embroidering, especially if it has been in a hoop for a prolonged period or has many directional stitches that tend to pull the work one way over another. Before finishing it into something such as a pillow or a frame, block the piece to stretch it back to its correct proportions, and square off the sides so that it is prepped for finishing.

First, gather your materials. You'll need a clean wooden board at least ¾" thick that is larger than your finished embroidery, a piece of sturdy white cotton fabric about 8" wider and longer than your piece of wood, a box of round-head 1" rustproof nails, a staple gun, staples, and a hammer.

Wrap the board with the cotton fabric, stapling all raw and folded edges to the underside of the wooden board.

Lay your finished embroidery faceup and centered on the board. Starting in the center of the top edge of your needlework, tack a nail through all layers into the board. Only about ¼" of the nail needs to go into the board. Smoothing the fabric with your hands and stretching it as necessary, tack another nail through the center of the bottom edge. Do the same in the center of the left and right edges. Working from the centers to the corners, alternating top to bottom and then left to right, nail the embroidery until all edges are

secured. The spaces between nails should be about 1". Be sure to keep the design square while you work. This may require stretching and pulling if your needlework lost its shape while you were embroidering. Then, spray the finished needlework with cold water until it is completely soaked. Set the board in a warm, airy place and let the needlework dry. If you're in a hurry, use a fan or cool hair dryer to speed up the process. When your work is dry, remove the nails with a hammer or pliers. Your work is now blocked and ready to be framed or sewn.

layering and binding a quilt

You may wish to finish some of your embroidery projects as quilts, such as the *Welcome Cottage* and *Halloween Queen* wall hangings on *pages 30* and *60*. Refer to the following instructions for layering and binding a quilt.

Cut and piece the backing fabric to measure at least 4" bigger on all sides than the quilt top. Press seams open. With wrong sides together, layer quilt top and backing fabric with batting in between; baste.

Binding for most quilts is cut on the straight grain of the fabric. Cutting instructions for the projects in this book specify the number of binding strips or a total length needed to finish the quilt. Instructions also specify enough width for a French-fold, or double-layer, binding because it's easier to apply and adds durability.

Join strips with diagonal seams to make one continuous binding strip (**Diagram 1**). Trim excess fabric, leaving ¼" seam allowances. Press seams open. Fold one end of the binding strip under 1" (**Diagram 2**); press. With wrong side inside, fold strip in half lengthwise and press (**Diagram 3**).

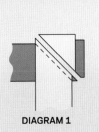

DIAGRAM 1

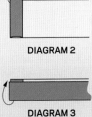

DIAGRAM 2

DIAGRAM 3

Beginning in the center of one edge, place binding strip against right side of quilt top, aligning binding strip's raw edges with quilt top's raw edge (Diagram 4). Sew through all layers, stopping ¼" (or a distance equal to the seam allowance you're using) from the corner. Backstitch, then clip threads. Remove quilt from under the sewing-machine presser foot.

DIAGRAM 4

Fold binding strip upward, creating a diagonal fold, and finger-press (Diagram 5).

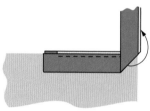

DIAGRAM 5

Holding the diagonal fold in place with your finger, bring binding strip down in line with next edge of quilt top, making a horizontal fold that aligns with the quilt edge (Diagram 6).

DIAGRAM 6

Start sewing again at top of horizontal fold, stitching through all layers. Sew around quilt, turning each corner in the same manner.

When you return to the starting point, encase binding strip's raw edge inside the folded end (Diagram 7). Finish sewing to the starting point (Diagram 8). Trim batting and backing fabric even with the quilt top edges.

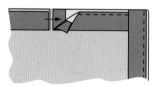

DIAGRAM 7

DIAGRAM 8

Turn binding over each edge to the back. Hand-stitch binding to backing fabric, making sure to cover all machine stitching.

To make mitered corners on the back, hand-stitch up to a corner; fold a miter in binding. Take a stitch or two in the fold to secure it. Then stitch the binding in place up to the next corner. Finish each corner in the same manner.

credits

PHOTOGRAPHERS
Adam Albright: page 126
Marty Baldwin: pages 10, 52, 64, 108, 114, 116, 122, 124, 130, 146
Kim Cornelison: pages 82, 140
Jason Donnelly: page 132
Blaine Moats: pages 38, 66

Donna Rickles: page 8
Cameron Sadeghpour: pages 36, 42, 74, 98, 118
Greg Scheidemann: pages 20, 30, 66, 78, 102, 134
Perry Struse: pages 16, 56, 60
Jay Wilde: pages 14, 70, 86, 92, 94